Frommer's®

D0338146

Maui
day BY day

1st Edition

by Jeanette Foster

1807
WILEY
2007
Wiley Publishing, Inc.

Contents

Published by:

Wiley Publishing, Inc.

111 River St.
Hoboken, NJ 07030-5774

ISBN-13: 978-0-470-05398-0
ISBN-10: 0-470-05398-4

Editor: Margot Weiss
Production Editor: Katie Robinson
Photo Editor: Richard Fox
Cartographer: Roberta Stockwell
Anniversary Logo Design: Richard Pacifico
Production by Wiley Indianapolis Composition Services

For information on our other products and services or to obtain technical support, please contact our Customer Care Department within the U.S. at 800/762-2974, outside the U.S. at 317/572-3993 or fax 317/572-4002.

Wiley also publishes its books in a variety of electronic formats. Some content that appears in print may not be available in electronic formats.

Manufactured in China

5   4   3   2   1

A Note from the Publisher

Organizing your time. That's what this guide is all about.

Other guides give you long lists of things to see and do and then expect you to fit the pieces together. The Day by Day guides are different. These guides tell you the best of everything, and then they show you how to see it *in the smartest, most time-efficient way.* Our authors have designed detailed itineraries organized by time, neighborhood or special interest. And each tour comes with a bulleted map that takes you from stop to stop.

Hoping to sunbathe on a secluded beach, or to explore Haleakala National Park? Planning on snorkeling Molokini, driving the winding road to Hana, or relaxing at one of Maui's beachside spas? Whatever your interest or schedule, the Day by Days give you the smartest route to follow. Not only do we take you to the top sights and attractions, but we introduce you to those special moments that only locals know about—those "finds" that turn tourists into travelers.

The Day by Days are also your top choice if you're looking for one complete guide for all your travel needs. The best hotels and restaurants for every budget, the greatest shopping values, the wildest nightlife—it's all here.

Why should you trust our judgment? Because our authors personally visit each place they write about. They're an independent lot who say what they think and would never include places they wouldn't recommend to their best friends. They're also open to suggestions from readers. If you'd like to contact them, please send your comments my way at mspring@wiley.com, and I'll pass them on.

Enjoy your Day by Day guide—the most helpful travel companion you can buy. And have the trip of a lifetime.

Warm regards,

Michael Spring
Publisher
Frommer's Travel Guides

About the Author

A resident of the Big Island, **Jeanette Foster** has skied the slopes of Mauna Kea—during a Fourth of July ski meet, no less—and gone scuba diving with manta rays off the Kona Coast. A prolific writer widely published in travel, sports, and adventure magazines, she's also a contributing editor to *Hawaii* magazine, the editor of *Zagat's Survey to Hawaii's Top Restaurants,* and the Hawaii chapter author of *1,000 Places to See Before You Die in the U.S. and Canada.* In addition to writing this guide, Jeanette is the author of *Frommer's Hawaii, Frommer's Hawaii from $80 a Day, Frommer's Kauai, Frommer's Hawaii with Kids, Frommer's Portable Big Island,* and *Frommer's Honolulu, Waikiki & Oahu.*

An Additional Note

Please be advised that travel information is subject to change at any time—and this is especially true of prices. We therefore suggest that you write or call ahead for confirmation when making your travel plans. The authors, editors, and publisher cannot be held responsible for the experiences of readers while traveling. Your safety is important to us, however, so we encourage you to stay alert and be aware of your surroundings.

Star Ratings, Icons & Abbreviations

Every hotel, restaurant, and attraction listing in this guide has been ranked for quality, value, service, amenities, and special features using a **star-rating system.** Hotels, restaurants, attractions, shopping, and nightlife are rated on a scale of zero stars (recommended) to three stars (exceptional). In addition to the star-rating system, we also use a **kids icon** to point out the best bets for families. Within each tour, we recommend cafes, bars, or restaurants where you can take a break. Each of these stops appears in a shaded box marked with a coffee-cup-shaped bullet 🍵.

The following **abbreviations** are used for credit cards:

AE	American Express	DISC	Discover	V	Visa
DC	Diners Club	MC	MasterCard		

Frommers.com

Now that you have this guidebook to help you plan a great trip, visit our website at **www.frommers.com** for additional travel information on more than 3,500 destinations. We update features regularly to give you instant access to the most current trip-planning information available. At Frommers.com, you'll find scoops on the best airfares, lodging rates, and car rental bargains. You can even book your travel online through our reliable travel booking partners.

A Note on Prices

In the Take a Break and Best Bets section of this book, we have used a system of dollar signs to show a range of costs for one night in a hotel (the price of a double-occupancy room) or the cost of an entrée at a restaurant. Use the following table to decipher the dollar signs:

Cost	Hotels	Restaurants
$	under $130	under $10
$$	$130–$200	$10–$20
$$$	$200–$300	$20–$30
$$$$	$300–$395	$30–$40
$$$$$	over $395	over $40

An Invitation to the Reader

In researching this book, we discovered many wonderful places—hotels, restaurants, shops, and more. We're sure you'll find others. Please tell us about them, so we can share the information with your fellow travelers in upcoming editions. If you were disappointed with a recommendation, we'd love to know that, too. Please write to:

Frommer's Maui Day by Day, 1st Edition
Wiley Publishing, Inc. • 111 River St. • Hoboken, NJ 07030-5774

16 Favorite
Moments

16 Favorite **Moments**

1. Hookipa Beach Park
2. The Road to Hana
3. Waianapanapa State Park
4. The Seven Sacred Pools
5. Haleakala National Park
6. Kula
7. Upcountry Maui
8. Molokini
9. Wailea
10. Whale-watching
11. Iao Valley
12. 13. Lahaina
14. West Maui Mountains
15. Kalaupapa
16. Lanai

To experience the true magic of Maui, just step outside to watch the glow of a sunrise, see the reflection of the moon on the inky ocean, sniff the perfume of flowers dancing in the air, or listen to the murmur of a tropical breeze through a bamboo forest. A few more of my favorite Maui experiences are described below.

1 **Watching windsurfers ride the waves at Hookipa.** This beach draws windsurfers and surfers from around the globe to ride, sail, and pirouette over the waves. Watching them flip into the air while rotating 360 degrees is the best free show in town. *See p 33.*

2 **Smelling the sweet scent of ginger on the road to Hana.** At every twist on this windy road you are greeted by exotic tropical blossoms, thundering waterfalls, breathtaking vistas, and a glimpse at what Maui looked like before it was "discovered." *See p 66.*

3 **Walking the shoreline trail at Waianapanapa.** This trail will take you back in time, past lava cliffs, a tropical forest, an ancient heiau (temple), mysterious caves, an exploding blowhole, native Hawaiian plants, and the ever-changing sea. *See p 71.*

4 **Taking a dip in the Seven Sacred Pools.** These fern-shrouded waterfall pools spill seaward at Oheo Gulch, on the rain-shrouded eastern flanks of Haleakala. *See p 73.*

5 **Greeting the rising sun from atop Haleakala.** Dress warmly and drive the 37 miles from sea level up to 10,000 feet, where you can watch the sunrise. Breathing in the rarefied air and watching the first rays of light streak across the sky is a mystical experience. *See p 84.*

6 **Heading to Kula to bid the sun aloha.** This town perched on the side of Haleakala is the perfect place to watch the sun set over the entire island, with vistas across the isthmus, the West Maui Mountains, and Molokai and Lanai in the distance. *See p 65.*

7 **Exploring Upcountry Maui.** On the slopes of Haleakala, cowboys, farmers, ranchers, and other country people make their serene, neighborly homes, worlds away from the bustling beach resorts. *See p 64.*

8 **Snorkeling off Molokini.** Calm, protected waters in the islet's crater, plus an abundance of marine life, make Molokini one of Hawaii's best places to snorkel. Paddle with turtles, watch clouds of butterfly fish flitter past, and search for tiny damselfish in the coral. *See p 102.*

Top surfer Laird Hamilton (left) at Hookipa Beach.

A beachside massage is the perfect way to relax.

9 Pampering in paradise. Maui's spas have raised the art of relaxation and healing to a new level. A massage on the beach will sooth out the kinks, while you bask in the sounds of the ocean, smell the salt air, and feel the caress of a warm breeze. *See p 36.*

10 Watching for whales. From mid-December through the end of March, humpback whales can be seen from shore jumping, breaching, and slapping their pectoral fins. *See p 107.*

11 Exploring Iao Valley. When the sun strikes Iao Valley in the West Maui Mountains, an almost ethereal light sends rays out in all directions. This really may be Eden. *See p 58.*

12 Visiting a historic port town. In the 1800s, whalers swarmed into Lahaina and missionaries fought to stem the spread of their sinful influence. Rediscover those wild whaling days for yourself. *See p 50.*

13 Experiencing Art Night in Lahaina. Every Friday, under a canopy of stars, the town's galleries open their doors and serve refreshments. Wander in to see what's going on in Maui's creative community. *See p 139.*

14 Flying over the remote West Maui Mountains. The only way to see the inaccessible, prehistoric West Maui Mountains is by helicopter. You'll glide low over razor-thin cliffs and flutter past sparkling waterfalls while descending into canyons and valleys. *See p 20.*

15 Riding a Mule to Kalaupapa. Even if you have only 1 day to spend on Molokai, spend it on a mule. Trek from "topside" Molokai down a narrow, dizzying switchback trail to Kalaupapa National Historic Park below. *See p 19.*

16 Taking a Day Trip to Lanai. Sailing from Lahaina Harbor, you can admire Maui from offshore, go snorkeling in the clear waters of Lanai, tour this tiny former plantation island, and still catch the last ferry back. *See p 152.* ●

Lahaina's harbor.

1 Strategies for Seeing **Maui**

Strategies for Seeing **Maui**

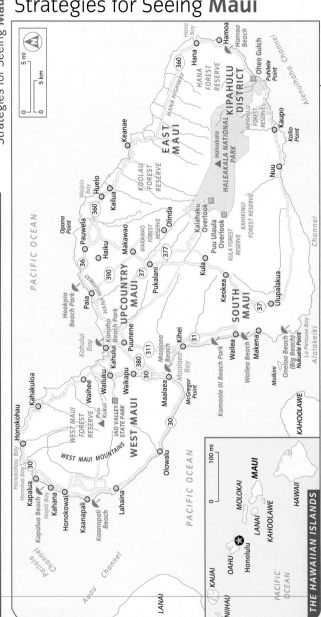

Maui may be an island, but it's a good-sized island and your vacation time is precious. There really is just one cardinal rule: relax. Maui is not a place to "see" but a place to experience. If you are too busy rushing to see everything, you won't experience the magic of the island. Here are my suggestions for making the most out of your time.

Rule #1: Remember you are on vacation

Don't jam-pack your days with activities; allow time to relax, to stop and smell the plumerias. Since you'll probably arrive jet lagged, make sure to spend some time on your first day lounging around the beach or the hotel swimming pool. Don't forget that exposure to sunlight can help reset your internal clock—another good reason to visit the beach when you arrive.

Rule #2: Driving takes a lot longer on Maui

You will need a car to get around; Maui does not have adequate public transportation. But plan to get out of your car as much as possible. Don't just look at Maui from the car window, get out and breath in the tropical aroma, soak in those views, and listen to the sounds of the island. Sure, you could drive the 50-mile- (80.5km-) long Hana Highway in as few as 2 to 3 hours, but that would miss the point of the journey entirely. One last thing: Maui does have traffic jams. Between 7 to 9am and 4 to 6pm the main roads are bumper-to-bumper with commuters. Plan accordingly. Sleep in late and get on the road after the traffic has cleared out, or watch the sunset and then go to dinner.

Rule #3: If your visit is short, stay in one place

Unless you're visiting for a week or longer, try not to hotel hop. With the exception of Hana, all the towns on Maui are within easy driving distance. Second, it is not easy (or cheap) checking in and out of hotels. There's the schlepping of the luggage (and the corresponding tips to the parking valet, the bellman, and so on), the waiting in line to check in, and unpacking, only to repeat the entire process a few days later. Your vacation time is too precious.

Rule #4: Pick the key activity of the day and plan accordingly

To maximize your time, decide what you really want to do that day, then plan all other activities in the same geographical area. For example, if you really want to go golfing at Kapalua, pick a beach in the same area for the afternoon or a shopping spree in the

Take some time to stop and smell the plumerias.

area and plan dinner nearby, that way you won't have to track back and forth across the island.

Rule #5: Remember you are on the island of aloha

Maui is different. Slow down (no need to rush, you're on vacation). Smile and say "aloha," it's what the local residents do. Ask them: "Howzit?" (the local expression for "how are you?"). When they ask you, tell 'em "Couldn't be better—I'm on Maui!" Wave at everyone—you'll feel better, they'll feel better. Laugh a lot, even if things aren't going as

Makena Beach.

Keep your eyes peeled, and you might see a Hawaiian honeycreeper like this one.

planned—laugh. Even if you're stuck in a traffic jam—laugh. (Hey, you're on Maui, how bad can it be?)

Rule #6: Use this book as a reference, not a concrete plan

You will not hurt my feelings if you don't follow every single tour and do absolutely everything I've suggested. In fact, you'll have a better time if you pick and choose the tours you want to take and the things you want to do. This book is filled with recommendations. ●

Fly Direct

If possible, fly non-stop and directly to the island of Maui (the airport is in Kahului and the airport code is OGG). Not only is it easier, but it will save you time. Yes, there are flights from the U.S. Mainland through Honolulu and then on to Maui, but the "on to Maui" bit generally means getting off a plane in the big, big Honolulu International Airport, and transferring to another terminal. Going through the fun-filled security procedures (taking off your shoes again!), and then checking in and waiting (sometimes up to 2 hours) for your flight to Maui is no way to begin a vacation.

The Best in Three Days

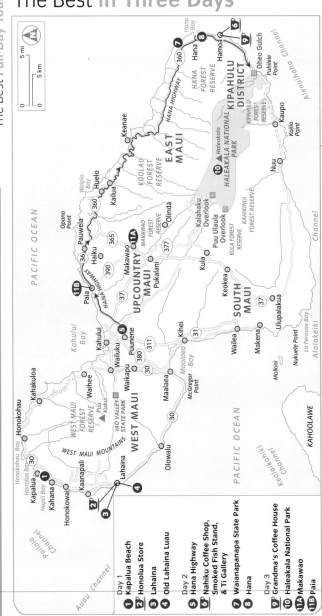

Day 1
1. Kapalua Beach
2. Honolua Store
3. Lahaina
4. Old Lahaina Luau

Day 2
5. Hana Highway
6. Nahiku Coffee Shop, Smoked Fish Stand, & Ti Gallery
7. Waianapanapa State Park
8. Hana

Day 3
9. Grandma's Coffee House
10. Haleakala National Park
11A. Makawao
11B. Paia

Maui may be an island, but it's a big one (48 miles by 26 miles/77km by 42km), the second largest of the Hawaiian Islands. If you only have 3 days, concentrate on the very best Maui has to offer: a beach, the scenic Hana Highway, and the view from the top of Haleakala, a 10,000-foot- (3,000km-) high dormant volcano. Try to spend your first night in conveniently located Lahaina-Kaanapali. Day 1 from the airport to your accommodations in Lahaina-Kaanapali and to the beach will total 40 miles (64.4km); day 2 to Hana will be 75 miles (120.75km); and day 3, from Hana to Haleakala and back to the airport, will be 87 miles (140km).

START: **Kapalua Beach. Trip length: 177-mile (285km) loop**

Travel Tip

For detailed descriptions of the beaches in this chapter, see chapter 5. For hotel reviews, see chapter 7. For more on the recommended restaurants, see chapter 8.

To get to Kapalua Beach from Lahaina/Kaanapali, take Hwy. 30 north to Kapalua. Go left at the Kapalua Resort sign on to Office Rd. and follow to the end. Take a left on Honoapiilai Rd. and another left at the beach access sign next door to the Napili Kai condominium.

❶ ★★★ **Kapalua Beach.** Check in to your hotel, then head for Kapalua Beach. Don't overdo the sun on your first day. Bring plenty of water, sunscreen, and a hat. The

Luxuriating in the warm sea and sun of Kapalua Beach.

adventurous might want to rent snorkel equipment, but those seeking a relaxing afternoon should simply lounge on the sand and enjoy the warm water. See p 79.

Retrace your route back to Hwy. 30 and turn right, continue into Lahaina town.

❷ **Honolua Store.** For a quick sandwich or a cold drink, I love this old-fashioned country general store, with surprisingly low prices. *502 Office Rd., just after the entrance to the Ritz-Carlton Kapalua. Breakfast, lunch & dinner daily.* ☎ *808/669-6128. $.*

❸ ★★★ **Lahaina.** After an hour or 2 at the beach, spend a couple of hours walking this historic old town, which at one time was the capital of Hawaii, a favorite spot for both whalers and missionaries. Today, not only can you enjoy the oceanfront village's historical past, but also its unique boutique shops, dozens of restaurants, and options for nightlife. See the walking tour on p 50 for more information.

❹ ★★★ **Old Lahaina Luau.** To really feel as though you are in Hawaii, attend this sunset luau and immerse yourself in the local culture. The luau begins at sunset and

Boats moored in Lahaina's harbor.

features Tahitian and Hawaiian entertainment. The food is as much Pacific Rim as authentically Hawaiian, from imu-roasted Kalua pig to baked mahimahi to teriyaki sirloin steak. *1251 Front St.,* ☎ *800/248-5828 or 808/667-1998; www.oldlahainaluau. com. $89 adults, $59 children 12 and under. See p 150.*

From Lahaina/Kaanapali take Hwy. 30 south to Hwy. 380 and turn right (east). In Kahului Hwy. 380 becomes Dairy Rd. Turn right (east) on Hwy. 36.

5 ★★★ Hana Highway. You'll probably wake up early on your first day in Hawaii, so take advantage of it and get out as quickly as you can

and onto the scenic Hana Highway. Allow at least 3½ to 5 hours for the journey. Pull over often, get out to take photos, smell the flowers, and jump in the mountain-stream pools. Wave to everyone, move off the road for those speeding by, and breathe in Hawaii. For a detailed description of this route, see p 66.

After MM 16, Hwy. 36 becomes Hwy. 360 and starts with mile marker 0. After about 1 to 1½ hours down the road, a ½ mile (0.8km) past MM 28 on the ocean side of the highway, you'll see:

6 Nahiku Coffee Shop. The small coffee shop sells delicious locally made baked goods, Maui-grown coffee, banana bread, organic tropical-fruit smoothies, and the Original and Best Coconut Candy made by Hana character Jungle Johnny.

Another 20 minutes down the road, just past MM 32:

7 Waianapanapa State Park. Just outside of Hana, stop at this state park and take a hike along the black sand beach. See p 90.

Maui Driving Tips

Hawaii residents know the highways by their Hawaiian names; very few know the highway number. I've included both the Hawaiian highway name and number on the maps, but the directions in this book mainly refer to the highway number. You'll also see the abbreviation MM, which stands for "mile marker." Below is a quick reference to the names and numbers of Maui's highways.

Hwy. 30: Honoapiilani Hwy.

Hwy. 31: Piilani Hwy.

Hwy. 36 & Hwy. 360: Hana Hwy.

Hwy. 37: Haleakala Hwy. & the Kula Hwy.

Hwy. 311: Mokulele Hwy.

Hwy. 377 & Hwy 378: Haleakala Hwy.

Hwy. 380: Kuihelani Hwy.

The dramatic black sands of Waiana-panapa State Park.

About ½ mile after MM 33 you come to the outskirts of Hana; veer left at the police and fire station on to Ua Kea Rd.

⑧ Hana. While you're here, make sure to hit three of my favorite spots, the **Hana Cultural Center and Museum,** the **Hasagawa General Store,** and **Hana Coast Gallery.** Spend the night in Hana. For more detailed information on Hana's sights, see p 70.

Allow at least 2 hours to get from Hana to the top of Haleakala. From Hana head west on Hwy. 31, which becomes Ulapalakua after Hwy. 37.

🍵 Grandma's Coffee House. I always order the homegrown Haleakala coffee and one of the fresh-baked pastries at this tiny wooden coffeehouse. *At the end of Hwy. 37, Keokea (about 6 miles/ 9.7km before the Tedeschi Vineyards in Ulupalakua).* ☎ *808/ 878-2140. www.grandmas coffee.com. Daily 7am–5pm. $.*

From Grandma's Coffee House, continue on Hwy. 37. Turn right on Hwy. 377 and then right again at Hwy. 378 to the top of Haleakala.

⑩ ★★★ Haleakala National Park. Leave Hana early and drive around the Kaupo side of Haleakala (stopping for a mid-morning snack at Grandma's Coffee House (see above), and then up the 10,000-foot (3,000km) (dormant) volcano, **Haleakala.** Although you won't have time on this trip to hike into the crater, spend an hour wandering around the park. See p 84 for details. ☎ *808/572-4400. www.nps. gov/hale. Daily from 7am–4pm.*

Retrace your steps back down Hwy. 378, then turn right on Hwy. 377 and right again on Hwy. 37. At the light turn right on Makawao Ave. and drive into the town of Makawao. To get to Paia from Makawao, head downhill on Baldwin Ave., which ends in Paia.

⑪ Makawao. Tour **Ⓐ** the **old cowboy town,** then plan a sunset dinner in **Ⓑ Paia** (see p 64), before heading back to the airport. See tours **⑪** & **⑫** for more information. See p 46.

From Hwy. 36 in Paia, drive to Kahului, turning right on Dairy Rd. and continuing on to Keolani Place and the airport.

The old cowboy town of Makawao.

The Best in One Week

THE HAWAIIAN ISLANDS

LANAI

Day 1
1A Kapalua Beach
1B Lahaina

Day 2
2 Lanai

Day 3
3 Haleakala National Park
4A Makawao
4B Paia

Day 4
5 Hana Highway

Day 5
6 Hana

Day 6
7 Ulupalakua
8 Haliimaile General Store

Day 7
9 Maui Ocean Center
10 Wailea
11 Iao Valley

Ideally, I recommend you stay at least a week on Maui to take in this sensuous island at a slow, leisurely pace. This weeklong itinerary adds a few new favorites to the 3-day tour: sailing to the island of Lanai; seeing the sharks and other ocean creatures at the Maui Ocean Center; and, depending on your preference, a final day on the beach, at a spa, or shopping for souvenirs. To avoid unnecessary driving I'd suggest staying in West Maui (Lahaina-Kaanapali-Kapalua) the first 3 nights, in Hana the next 3 nights, and in South Maui (Kihei-Wailea) on the last night. START: **Kapalua Beach. Trip Length: 247½ miles (398.5km)**

Travel Tip

West Maui is the area from Lahaina north including: Kaapanali, Honokowai, Kahana, Napili, and Kapalua. South Maui includes Kihei, Wailea, and Makena.

To get to Kapalua Beach from West Maui, drive north on Hwy. 30 to Kapalua. Turn left at the Kapalua Resort sign on Office Rd.; go to the end of the road. Left on Honoapiilai Rd., and turn into the beach access sign next door to the Napili Kai condominium.

1A ★★★ Kapalua Beach & 1B Lahaina. For detailed suggestions on how to make the most of your first day, see Day 1 in "The Best of Maui in Three Days" (p 11).

Go south on Hwy. 30 to Lahaina. Turn right at the light on Dickenson St. Look for the Republic Parking sign on the right. Allow ½ hour from Kapalua and 15 minutes from Kaanapali.

2 ★★★ Lanai. Get out on the water early with **Trilogy** (p 103) my favorite sailing/snorkeling trip in Hawaii. You'll spend the morning (breakfast and lunch included) sailing to the island of Lanai, touring the island, and sailing back to Lahaina. In the afternoon you can go shopping for souvenirs or relax. For dinner, I'd book a table on the roof at sunset at the **Lahaina Store Grille and Oyster Bar** (p 128), followed by the drama/dance/music show, **'Ulalena** (p 149).

Check your brakes before racing down Haleakala on a bike.

Take Hwy. 30 south. Turn right on Hwy. 380, right again on Hwy. 36, then another right on Hwy. 37. Just after Pukalani, turn left on Hwy. 377. Turn left again at the sign to the Haleakala National Park on Hwy. 378 and take it to the top. The summit is 40 to 50 miles (64.4–80.5km) from West Maui. Allow at least 2 hours.

❸ ★★★ Haleakala National Park. Head up the 10,000-foot- (3,000m-) high dormant volcano, Haleakala. You can hike in the crater (p 89), speed down the mountain on a bicycle (p 97), or simply wander about the park. You don't have to be at the top for sunrise, but I have to tell you—it is a near-religious experience you'll never forget. ☎ *808/572-4400. www.nps.gov/hale. Daily from 7am–4pm.*

Retrace your route down the mountain via highways 378, 377, and 37, and turn right at the light on Makawao Ave. To get to Paia from Makawao, head downhill on Baldwin Ave., which ends in Paia.

❹A Makawao & ❹B Paia. See p 13 ⓫.

To return to West Maui take Hwy. 30 north towards the Kahului Airport and turn left on Dairy Rd., which becomes Hwy. 380. Turn left on Hwy. 30 all the way to Lahaina/Kaanapali. The trip is about 30 to 40 miles (48.3–64.4km) and takes at least 1 to 1½-hours.

❺ ★★★ Hana Highway. See p 12 ❺.

❻ ★★★ Hana. Since you have the entire day to spend, in addition to the suggestions on p 13 ❽, I also recommend checking out **Hamoa** or **Red Sand** beaches (see chapter 5); snorkeling or kayaking (rent equipment from **Hana-Maui Sea Sports,** see p 106), or touring one of the largest ancient Hawaiian temples in

Tedeschi Winery's tasting room.

the state, **Piilanihale Heiau,** see p 71. Spend another night in Hana.

Get on the road by 10am for Day 6. Head west on Hwy. 31 to Ulupalakua, allowing at least 1 hour driving time.

❼ Ulupalakua. As you continue driving around the island, make sure to stop at the **Ulupalakua Ranch** and the **Tedeschi Winery** (see p 65 ❹) in Ulupalakua. I generally can't resist getting a cup of java at **Grandma's Coffee House,** see p 13 ❾.

After Ulapalakua, Hwy. 31 is called Hwy. 37. Take Hwy. 37 north, then turn right on Haliimaile Rd. The drive takes 30 to 40 minutes.

Heading down the mountain, stop for lunch in the middle of the pineapple fields at the ❽ **Haliimaile General Store,** p 126.

Get back on Hwy. 37 heading downhill, and turn right. Turn left at the intersection of Hwy. 36, and left again on Dairy Rd., which becomes Hwy. 380. When the road ends, turn left on Hwy. 30;

the left turn to Maalaea comes up in less than a mile. The Maui Ocean Center is at the entrance to the village. The drive will take 30 to 40 minutes.

⑨ Maui Ocean Center. Spend the afternoon checking out the marine life, especially the sharks, in this marvelous aquarium. Since tomorrow's itinerary is in South Maui, Wailea, I'd suggest staying in Wailea tonight. For more information, see p 26 **⑦**. *Maalaea Harbor Village, 192 Maalaea Rd.* ☎ *808/270-7000. www.mauiocean center.com.*

To get to South Maui from Maalaea, turn right on Hwy. 30, then right on Hwy. 31. To get to Wailea Beach from South Maui (allow 15 minutes from the north end of Kihei), take Hwy. 31 south, which ends on Wailea Iki Dr. At the stop sign (note the Shops at Wailea straight ahead), turn left on Wailea Alanui Rd. and look for the blue shoreline access sign, which will take you to a public parking lot.

Wailea Beach.

Iao Valley.

⑩ Wailea. Depending on how much time you have on your final day, you can choose from relaxing on the beach, snorkeling with tropical fish, being pampered in a spa, or shopping. I never pass up an opportunity to go to my favorite beach in South Maui, **Wailea Beach** (p 82), fronting the Four Seasons Maui and the Grand Wailea resorts (you don't have to stay at these resorts to use the beach). Spa goers have a range of terrific **spas** to choose from (p 36) and shopping aficionados should check out some of my favorite stores at the nearby **Shops at Wailea** (p 142).

To go from Wailea Beach to Iao Valley, head north on Hwy. 31 and turn right on Hwy. 30. In the town of Wailuku, turn left at the light on to Main St., which becomes Iao Valley Rd., and ends at Iao Valley State Park. The 8-mile (12.9km) trip will take about 30 to 40 minutes.

⑪ Iao Valley. If you have a late flight, you might want to spend some time in this historic area on your way back to the airport. See p 58 **②**.

The Best in Two Weeks

Day 1
1 Kapalua Beach

Day 2
2 Lanai

Day 3
3 Lahaina

Day 4
4A Haleakala National Park
4B Makawao
4C Paia

Day 5
5 Molokai Mule Ride

Day 6
6A Blue Hawaiian Helicopter
6B Wailuku town
6C Iao Valley
6D Halekii and Pihanakalani
6E Kahekili Highway
6F Kahakuloa

Day 7
7 Hana Highway

Day 8
8 Hana

Day 9
9 Ulupalakua

10 Haliimaile General Store

Day 9 / Day 10
11 Maui Ocean Center

Day 10
12 Wailea

Day 11
13 Molokini

Day 12
14 Up-Country Farm Tours

Day 13
15 Makena

Day 14
16 Kihei

Two weeks on Maui separates the visitors from the adventurers and gives you time to really get to know this exotic isle. The tour is similar to Maui in 1 week with a few additional stops: flying to Molokai and riding a mule into the dramatic Kalaupapa Peninsula; seeing Maui from a helicopter; driving around the backside of Maui; snorkeling in the old volcanic crater of Molokini; touring Maui's farms; and kayaking off historic Makena. To reduce driving time, plan on spending 6 nights in West Maui, 2 nights in Hana, and 5 nights in South Maui. START: **Kapalua Beach. End: Kihei. Trip length: 538 miles (866.2km)**

1A ★★★ **Kapalua Beach.** See **1** in the Best of Maui in Three Days, starting on p 11.

2 Lanai. See **2** in The Best of Maui in One Week on p 15.

Turn right on Hwy. 30 to Lahaina town.

3 ★★ **Lahaina.** Plan to arrive in this historic town early, before the crowds. I recommend **Lahaina Coolers** (p 128) for a big breakfast, then put on your walking shoes and take the self-guided **historic walking tour** of the old town (p 50), do some browsing in the quaint stores (p 134), watch the surfers skim the waves in front of the library, and pop over to Kaanapali to the **Whale Center of the Pacific** (p 49).

Take Hwy. 30 south. Turn right on Hwy. 380, right again on Hwy. 36, then another right on Hwy. 37. Just after Pukalani, turn left on

Hwy. 377. Turn left again at the sign to the Haleakala National Park on Hwy. 378 and take it to the top. The summit is 40 to 50 miles (64.4–80.5km) from West Maui. Allow at least 2 hours.

4A ★★★ **Haleakala National Park.** For details on exploring this volcano, plus the rural towns of **4B** **Makawao** and **4C** **Paia,** see **11** in the Best of Maui in Three Days starting on p 13.

To take the ferry to Molokai from Lahaina Harbor, take Hwy. 30 south to Lahaina. At the light at Dickenson St., turn right. Park, and walk toward the ocean to Front St. After the library, turn toward the ocean to the harbor.

5 ★★★ **Molokai Mule Ride.** For an unforgettable all-day adventure on the "Friendly Isle" take a mule ride into the **Kalaupapa**

Haleakala's crater.

Riding a mule on Molokai.

Peninsula. Starting at the top of the nearly perpendicular ridge (1,600-ft. high), Buzzy Sproat's surefooted mules step down the narrow, muddy 3-mile (4.8km) trail daily, rain or shine, pausing often on the 26 switchbacks to calculate their next move—and always, it seems to me, veering a little too close to the edge. Each switchback is numbered; by the time you get to number four, you'll catch your breath, put the mule on cruise control, and begin to enjoy Hawaii's most awesome trail ride. With a minimum of 2 people, you can also arrange to fly over for the day for an additional fee. ⏱ *7.5 hours. 100 Kalae Hwy., Suite 104, on Highway 470, 5 miles (8km) north of Highway 460.* ☎ *800/567-7550; www.muleride.com. Tours are offered daily starting at 8am and last until about 3:30pm. $165 per person. Riders must be at least 16 years old and physically fit.*

To get to the Heliport, head out on Hwy. 30, turn right on Hwy. 380, which becomes Dairy Rd. Turn right at the intersection of Hwy. 37. You will circle around the airport runway. Make a left on Leleipio Place.

Travel Tip—Rush Hour

Set out early or late to avoid Maui's rush hour, which lasts from 7 to 9am and from 4 to 6pm. Roads can be packed bumper-to-bumper—not a fun way to spend your vacation!

6A ★★★ See Maui from Above in a Helicopter. Floating over Maui in a helicopter will give you an entirely different perspective of the island, and of all the helicopter companies, I think **Blue Hawaiian Helicopter** (p 97) offers the most comfortable, informative, and fun tours. After your flight, head to Wailuku Town by retracing your steps back to Hwy. 37. Continue on 37 where it merges with Hwy. 36. Follow 36 until it merges with Hwy. 32 (Kaahumanu Ave), which will take you into Wailuku (the street changes its name to Main St. in Wailuku). Take some time to explore the old town of **6B Wailuku** (see the walking tour on p 58), wandering through the shops and stopping at the Bailey House on W. Main St. Continue on Main St., which changes its name to Iao Valley Rd., to the end where you will be in **6C Iao Valley** (p 58). From here, retrace your route back to Main St. Make a left on Market St., then a right on Mill St., which ends at Lower Main St., turn left and then left again on to Waiheu Beach Rd. (Hwy. 340). Go left on Kuhio Place and then take your first left on Hea Place. At the end of the street are the ancient temples of **6D Halekii** and **Pihanakalani**. If you aren't too tired, return to West Maui via the **6E Kahekili Highway.** Get here by retracing your route back to Waiheu Beach Rd. (Hwy. 340) and turning left. When the road ends, make a right on Kahekili Hwy. (Hwy. 340), stopping to see the ancient Hawaiian village of **6F Kahakuloa** (12

Molokini's distinctive crescent is the perfect haven for colorful, tropical fish.

miles/19.3km down the windy road) and then continue on to Lahaina, another 21 miles/33.8km away. For more on the temples, Kahekili Highway, and Kahakuloa, see the History & Culture tour on p 44.

To reach Hana Hwy. from Lahaina/Kaanapali, take Hwy. 30 south to Hwy. 380 and turn right (east). In Kahului Hwy. 380 becomes Dairy Rd. Turn right (east) on Hwy. 36.

Travel Tip

The next leg of your trip will follow the recommendations in "The Best of Maui in One Week." Start with **5** p 16 (Hana Hwy.) and follow the directions and recommendations through **10** p 17 (Wailea).

Viewing Maui from a helicopter.

7 **Hana Highway.** See p 66 **5**.

8 ★★★ **Hana.** See p 70 **6**.

9 **Ulupalakua.** See p 65 **7**.

10 Haliimaile General Store. See p 16 **8**.

11 **Maui Ocean Center.** See p 17 **9**.

To reach Wailea, see directions on p 17.

12 **Wailea.** A great place to relax on the beach, get pampered at a spa or go shopping. See p 17 **10**.

The boat trip to Molokini departs from Maalaea Harbor: travel on Hwy. 31 north, turn left on Hwy. 30. The left-turn exit to Maalaea comes up within a mile.

13 ★★★ **Molokini.** Take a day to see the fish inside the Molokini Crater. Go in the morning before the wind comes up. If it's whale season and you're lucky, you may spot whales on the way over or back. I recommend taking one of **Trilogy's** tours (see p 103).

Depending on traffic, allow at least an hour to drive from South Maui to the Alii Kula Lavender Farm. Take Hwy. 31 north to Hwy. 311 and turn right. At the light on Hwy. 380, turn right on Dairy Rd. Turn right on to Hwy. 37, and follow it up the mountain to Kula. Take the second left after Rice Park onto Kekauliki Ave. Drive about ¼ mile, rounding a bend, taking a quick right up Waipoli Rd. From the Lavender Farm to the Surfing Goat Dairy, retrace your route to the Kula Highway. About 3 miles (4.8km) along the Kula Hwy., make a left down Omaopio Rd. In about 3 miles (4.8km) you'll see the farm sign on the left.

14 Up-Country Farm Tours.

Plan at least one off-the-beaten-path tour while you're on Maui. For a really exotic experience, plus terrific food, take the **Garden and Culinary Tour of the Alii Kula Lavender Farm** (see 4C, p 32), which includes a tour of the farm and lunch made with lavender products. Cheese aficionados will love the **Surfing Goat Dairy tour** (see 3, p 40) and the sampling of their cheeses.

To get to Makena Beach on Day 13, take Hwy. 31 south, which ends at Wailea Ike Dr. Turn left at the intersection onto Wailea Alanui Rd., which becomes Makean Alanui Rd. Turn right on Makena Rd. to Makena Bay. From there to La Pérouse Bay continue on Makena Rd. until it ends, then take off on foot for a couple of miles to reach the bay.

Kayaking in La Pérouse Bay near the Ahihi-Kinau Natural Preserve.

One of Kihei's beaches.

15 Makena.
Kayaking is so easy here that you'll be paddling away within a few minutes of taking a lesson. It's calm, the water is clear enough that you can see the fish, and you are protected from the wind (see "Kayak Tours" on p 106). After a couple of hours of kayaking and snorkeling, stop for a picnic lunch at **Makena Landing**, then explore this area. If you have some energy to spare, hike over to **La Pérouse Bay,** along the rugged shoreline, and see the Ahihi-Kinau Natural Preserve on p 101.

Head north on South Kihei Rd.

16 Kihei.
After 13 days of exploring Maui, spend your last day doing whatever you love best, whether it's beach-hopping the 5 miles (8km) of white-sand beaches that line the town of Kihei (p 56), beachcombing, snorkeling, or shopping. Pick up a lei at the Kmart on Dairy Rd. near the airport before you fly out so you will have a little bit of Maui with you as you say aloha. ●

3 The Best Special-Interest Tours

Maui with Kids

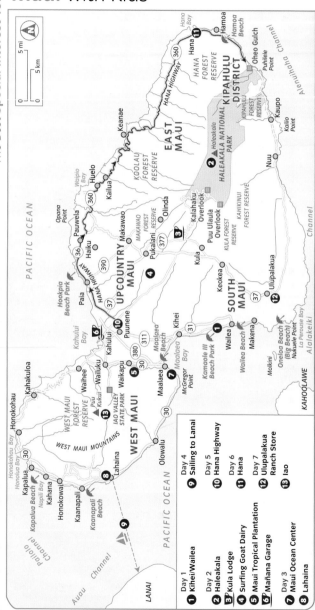

N

0 ____ 5 mi
0 ____ 5 km

PACIFIC OCEAN

HANA HIGHWAY 360

Hana Bay

Hamoa

Hamoa Beach

Oheo Gulch

Puhilele Point

Alenuihaha Channel

HANA FOREST RESERVE

KIPAHULU DISTRICT

KIPAHULU FOREST RESERVE

Kaupo

Kalio Point

Keanae

EAST MAUI

KOOLAU FOREST RESERVE

Haleakala

HALEAKALA NATIONAL PARK

Kalahaku Overlook

Puu Ulaula Overlook

KAHIKINUI FOREST RESERVE

Nuu

Channel

Waipio Bay

Huelo

Kailua

Opana Point

Pauwela

Haiku

Makawao

Olinda

MAKAWAO FOREST RESERVE

Pukalani

Kula

KULA FOREST RESERVE

Keokea

Ulupalakua

SOUTH MAUI

Hookipa Beach Park

Paia

UPCOUNTRY MAUI

Kahului Bay

Puunene

Kihei

Wailea

Kamaole III Beach Park

Wailea Beach

Makena

Molokini

Oneloa Beach (Big Beach)
Nukuele Point

La Perouse Bay

Alalakeiki Channel

KAHOOLAWE

Kahului

Wailuku

Waikapu

Maalaea

Maalaea Bay

McGregor Point

Kahakuloa

Waihee

WEST MAUI FOREST RESERVE

Puu Kukui

IAO VALLEY STATE PARK

WEST MAUI MOUNTAINS

WEST MAUI

Olowalu

Honokohau

Honokohau Bay

Honolua Bay

Kapalua

Napili Bay

Kapalua Beach

Kahana

Honokowai

Kaanapali

Kaanapali Beach

Lahaina

Pailolo Channel

Auau Channel

LANAI

PACIFIC OCEAN

Day 1
1 Kihei/Wailea

Day 2
2 Haleakala
3 Kula Lodge
4 Surfing Goat Dairy
5 Maui Tropical Plantation
6 Mañana Garage

Day 3
7 Maui Ocean Center
8 Lahaina

Day 4
9 Sailing to Lanai

Day 5
10 Hana Highway

Day 6
11 Hana

Day 7
12 Ulupalakua Ranch Store
13 Iao

Your itinerary is going to depend on the ages of your kids. The number-one rule is *don't plan too much*, especially with young children, who will be fighting jet lag, trying to get adjusted to a new bed (and most likely new food), and may be hyped up to the point of exhaustion. The 7-day itinerary below is a guide to the various family-friendly activities available on Maui; I'd suggest staying in South Maui (Kihei or Wailea) for the first 2 nights, then moving to West Maui (Lahaina or Kaanapali) for the next 2 nights, and then to Hana for your last 2 nights. START: **Kihei/Wailea. Trip Length: 7 days and 295 miles (475km)**

Travel Tip

See chapter 7 for hotel recommendations and chapter 8 for detailed reviews of the restaurants mentioned in this chapter.

1 Kihei/Wailea. In my experience, the first thing kids want to do is hit the water. A great, safe beach to start with is **Wailea** (p 82), fronting the Four Seasons and the Grand Wailea Resorts. If you have young kids who are not used to the waves, you might consider taking them to the swimming pool at your hotel. They'll be happy playing in the water, and you won't have to introduce them to ocean safety

After a long plane ride, the beach is a great first stop for kids and adults.

after that long plane ride. If this is your first day in Maui, you'll probably want an early dinner, with food your kids are used to. My pick of family-friendly eateries in Kihei are either **Shaka Sandwiches and Pizza** (p 130) or **Stella Blues Cafe** (p 130). Get to bed early.

Allow 1½ to 2 hours to reach the Haleakala summit from South Maui. Go north on Hwy. 31 to Hwy. 311, then go right on Hwy. 36 and right again on Hwy. 37. Then take Hwy. 377 to Hwy. 378.

2 ★★★ Haleakala. Your family will probably be up early, so take advantage and head up to the 10,000-foot dormant volcano Haleakala. Depending on the age of your children, you can either **hike in the crater, speed down the mountain on a bicycle,** or just wander about the park. See chapter 6 for details. ☎ 808/572-4400. *www.nps.gov/hale. Daily from 7am–4pm.*

3 Kula Lodge. Depending on how hungry your kids are, I'd suggest taking them to breakfast here either on the way to or from Haleakala.

From the summit, allow 45 minutes to retrace Hwy. 378 to Hwy. 377, to Hwy. 37 and turn left onto Omaopio Rd. Look for the Surfing

The train ride through Maui Tropical Plantation.

Goat Dairy sign on the left about 2 miles (3.2km) down.

4 Surfing Goat Dairy. The kids (yours) will love petting and playing with the other kids (the goat variety). Don't leave without sampling their selection of cheeses. For more information, see p 40.

Continue down the mountain, taking a left on Hwy. 36 and continuing through Kahului and Wailuku. Go left on Hwy. 30. It should take you about 35 to 45 minutes.

5 Maui Tropical Plantation. This plantation in Waikapu offers a 40-minute tram ride through exotic flora and fruit that will amuse even jaded teenagers. See p 39.

6 Mañana Garage. Tonight I recommend another early dinner; Mañana Garage in Kahului has "garage decor" to keep the kids entertained and margaritas to remind you that you're on vacation. See p 128.

Take Hwy. 31 north and go left on Hwy. 30 to Maalaea. Depending on the location of your accommodations, allow about 30 minutes.

7 ★★★ Maui Ocean Center. After a lazy breakfast, wander over here so your kids can see the fabulous underwater world of sharks, stingrays, and starfish, without having to get wet. Plan to spend the morning immersed in the 5-acre oceanarium, then have lunch at the

A Great Way to Spend a Rainy Day

If it rains during your vacation, take the kids to the **Art School at Kapalua** (☎ 808/665-0007; www.kapaluamaui.com), which offers inexpensive classes, projects, and workshops in a charming 1920s plantation building. The school features local and visiting instructors, and is open daily for people of all ages and skill levels. This not-for-profit organization highlights creativity in all forms, including photography, figure drawing, ceramics, landscape painting, painting on silk, and the performing arts (ballet, yoga, creative movement, Pilates). Call to see what's scheduled.

center's **Reef Café.** ⏱ *2 to 3 hours. Maalaea Harbor Village, 192 Maalaea Rd., Maalaea.* ☎ *808/ 270-7000; www.mauioceancenter. com. Daily 9am–5pm.*

Head north on Hwy. 30 to Lahaina. The drive takes about 20 to 30 minutes.

8 Lahaina. In Lahaina you can take the kids underwater in a Jules Verne–type fantasy, the **Atlantis Submarine,** 658 Front St. (☎ 800/ 548-6262 or 808/667-7816; www.go atlantis.com. You'll plunge 100 feet under the sea in a state-of-the-art, high-tech submarine and meet swarms of vibrant tropical fish up close and personal as they flutter through the deep blue waters. Atlantis offers trips out of Lahaina Harbor every hour on the hour from 9am to 2pm; $84 for adults and $42 for children under 12 (children must be at least 3 ft. tall). Book on their website and save 10%. Allow 2 hours for this underwater adventure. Younger kids may prefer the

The Road to Hana is punctuated by spectacular waterfalls.

Maui Ocean Center.

Lahaina–Kaanapali Sugar Cane Train (☎ 808/661-0089; www. sugarcanetrain.com). Kids of all ages will enjoy hitting one of the terrific **beaches** on West Maui (see chapter 5) and maybe renting some snorkel equipment. Book ahead for the **Old Lahaina Luau** (p. 150) in the evening. Plan to spend the night in Lahaina.

In Lahaina, turn toward the ocean at the light on Dickenson St. Look for the Republic Parking sign, on the right.

9 ★★★ Sailing to Lanai. Trilogy (p 103) is the best sailing/snorkeling trip in Hawaii, so don't miss it. In the afternoon, wander around Lahaina (p 50) and hit a few kid-friendly highlights, including the giant **banyan tree,** the **Old Lahaina Courthouse,** and the old **Prison.** In the evening, older kids may be interested in checking out the night skies with a computer-driven telescope. Contact the Hyatt Regency Maui (☎ 800/233-1234 or 808/661-1234; www.maui.hyatt.com) to learn about their **Star Searches.**

Go south on Hwy. 30, right on Hwy. 380, and right on Hwy. 36 to Hana. With stops, this drive can take up to a whole day.

Family-Friendly Events

Your trip may be a little more enjoyable with the added attraction of attending a celebration, festival or party on Maui. Check out the following events:

- **Chinese New Year,** Lahaina (☎ 888/310-1117). Feb. 18, 2007 starts the year of the pig and Lahaina rolls out the red carpet with a traditional lion dance, accompanied by fireworks, food booths, and a host of activities..
- **Whale Day Celebration,** Kalama Park, Kihei (☎ 808/249-8811; www.visitmaui.com). In early to mid-February, this daylong celebration features a parade of whales, entertainment, a crafts fair, games, and food.
- **Ocean Arts Festival,** Lahaina (☎ 888/310-1117; www.visit lahaina.com). Kids will love this mid-March event with marine-related activities, games, and a touch-pool exhibit for children.
- **Annual Lei Day Celebration,** islandwide (☎ 808/875-4100; www.visitmaui.com). May Day is Lei Day in Hawaii, celebrated with lei-making contests, pageantry, arts and crafts, and concerts.
- **King Kamehameha Celebration,** islandwide (☎ 888/310-1117; www.visitlahaina.com). June 10 is a state holiday with a massive floral parade, *hoolaulea* (party), and much more.
- **Fourth of July.** Lahaina (☎ 888/310-1117; www.visitlahaina.com) holds an old-fashioned Independence Day celebration with fireworks. Kaanapali (☎ 808/661-3271) puts on a grand old celebration with live music, children's activities, and fireworks.
- **Maui County Fair,** War Memorial Complex, Wailuku, (☎ 800/525-MAUI; ww.calendarmaui.com) At the end of September, this traditional county fair features a parade, amusement rides, live entertainment, and exhibits.
- **Halloween in Lahaina** (☎ 888/310-1117; www.visitlahaina.com). There's Carnival in Rio, Mardi Gras in New Orleans, and Halloween in Lahaina. Some 20,000 people show up at this giant costume party.

The Atlantis Submarine.

⑩ ★★★ **Hana Highway.** Pack a lunch and spend the day driving the unforgettable Hana Highway. Pull over often and let the kids get out to take photos, smell the flowers, and jump in the mountain-stream pools. Plan to spend at least 2 nights in Hana. See p 66 for details.

⑪ ★★★ **Hana.** An entire day in paradise, with so many things to do. Take an early-morning hike along the black sands of **Waianapanapa State Park,** then explore the tiny town of Hana. Make sure you see the **Hana Cultural Center and Museum,** the **Hasagawa General Store,** and the **Hana Coast Gallery.** Get a picnic lunch and drive out to the Kipihulu end of Haleakala National Park at **Oheo Gulch.** Hike to the waterfalls, swim in the pools, take lots of photos. Splurge on dinner and eat at the dining room at the **Hotel Hana-Maui** (p 115). See p 70 for a detailed tour of Hana.

Continue past Hana on Hwy. 31 to Ulupalakua, allowing 45 minutes to an hour.

⑫ **Ulupalakua Ranch Store.** By the time you get to the Upcountry town of Ulupalakua, the kids will be restless. This eclectic general store, which dates back to 1849, is a good place for you all to stretch your legs—you can also grab lunch at the small deli inside. See p 65.

Hiking in Waianapanapa State Park.

Go north on Hwy. 37 and left on Hwy. 36 through Kahului and Wailuku. Continue straight at the light at Main St./Hwy. 30 and follow Iao Valley Rd. to its end. The drive will take 45 to 60 minutes.

⑬ **Iao.** If you have some time before your flight home, I'd recommend spending the afternoon at the **Hawaii Nature Center,** 875 Iao Valley Rd. (☎ 808/244-6500; www.hawaiinaturecenter.org), which has some 30 interactive exhibits on nature. Don't miss the Rainforest Walk, a moderate loop trail through the ancient footpaths in **Iao Valley** (p 58 ②). This guided walk includes commentary on native Hawaiian plants, the remains of ancient habitation, and stories of old Hawaii.

Romantic Maui

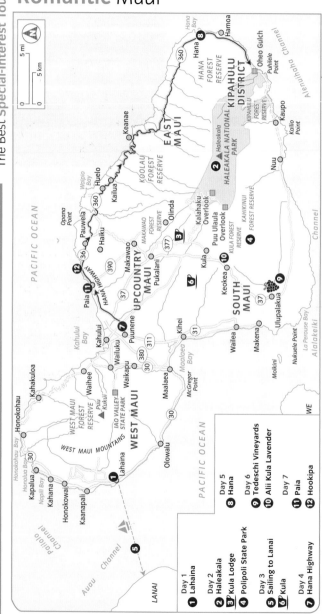

Day 1
1 Lahaina

Day 2
2 Haleakala
3 Kula Lodge
4 Polipoli State Park

Day 3
5 Sailing to Lanai
6 Kula

Day 4
7 Hana Highway

Day 5
8 Hana

Day 6
9 Tedeschi Vineyards
10 Alii Kula Lavender

Day 7
11 Paia
12 Hookipa

Maui's sensual side makes it the perfect place to fall in love. The smell of flowers in the air, the sound of the waves rolling in, and the island's exotic beauty all beckon lovers. If you're discovering Maui as a twosome, I suggest spending the first 3 nights in Lahaina, the next 2 in Hana, and your last night in the Upcountry area. START: **Lahaina. Trip Length: 7 days and 333 miles (536.1km)**

❶ Lahaina. Don't leave the Kahului Airport without giving your sweetie a sweet-smelling flower lei. Book my favorite Hawaii experience, the **Old Lahaina Luau** (see p 150), where the two of you can watch the sunset while enjoying a mai tai and a meal.

Allow 2 hours to drive to the summit of Haleakala. Head south on Hwy. 30, then go right on Hwy. 380, right on Hwy. 36, and right again on Hwy. 37. Then follow Hwy. 377 to Hwy. 378.

❷ Haleakala. If you've just arrived and are still on mainland time, make the most of it and get up early to drive to Haleakala National Park in time for the sunrise on the summit of this dormant volcano. The two of you, wrapped in a blanket (it's cold at 10,000 feet/3,000m), watching the stars slowly fade and the dim rays of dawn appear, will become one of your fondest memories. See p 84.

A selection of sweet-smelling flower lei.

Stop at **❸ Kula Lodge** for a big breakfast overlooking the isthmus of Maui. Get a takeout picnic lunch before you leave. See p 128. *$$.*

Head down Hwy. 378, then take a left on Hwy. 377 and go left on Waipoli Rd. to the end. To return to Lahaina, retrace back, left on Hwy. 377, right on Hwy. 30, and return to Lahaina.

❹ Polipoli State Park. In Polipoli you can walk in total silence (except for the sounds of the native birds) among the pine, redwood, and eucalyptus trees. You probably won't see another soul in this 21,000 acre forest reserve. Have a picnic, take a nap, and return to Lahaina for another sunset dinner, this one at the **Old Lahaina Store and Oyster Bar,** 744 Front St. (☎ 808/661-9090). See p 128.

In Lahaina, turn toward the ocean at the light on Dickenson St. Look for the sign: Republic Parking, on the right side of the street.

❺ ★★★ Sailing to Lanai. Nothing is more romantic than the wind kissing your face and the sun warming your skin as the two of you sail offshore to Lanai with **Trilogy** (p 103), my favorite sailing company. On the half-day excursion they hand you hot cinnamon rolls and coffee as soon as you step on board, and after the 9-mile (14.5km) trip to Lanai they'll take you on an island excursion and serve you a barbeque lunch.

Drive south on Hwy. 30, go right on Hwy. 380, right on Hwy. 36, and right again on Hwy. 37 to Rice Park. Allow about an hour from Lahaina to Kula.

Gather up the ingredients for a picnic dinner (I like **Moana Bakery & Café;** see p 129) and drive up to Harold W. Rice Memorial Park in **6** **Kula** to see the sunset. For a truly magical evening, linger over a bottle of wine or dessert until the stars come out.

From Lahaina, go south on Hwy. 30, turn right on Hwy. 380, then turn right on Hwy. 36 toward Hana. With stops, this drive will take a whole day.

7 **Hana Highway.** Bring your swim suit, put the top down, and turn the radio up—plan on spending the entire day cruising Maui's most famous curvy road. Stop at waterfalls, go for a swim in tranquil pools, pack a picnic, and enjoy every spontaneous moment. See p 66 for details.

8 **Hana.** Lush, tropical Hana is the perfect place for romance and it's well worth spending a couple of nights here. If you're ready for some relaxing beach time, you can choose the fiery red beach at **Red Sand Beach** (p 81), the perfect crescent white-sand bay at **Hamoa Beach** (p 78), or the freshwater pools at **Oheo Gulch,** where you can sit and soak while watching the waves rolling into shore. Around sunset, walk the ancient Hawaii trail at

The Road to Hana.

Splitting a bottle of wine at Tadeschi Vineyards is a wonderful way to while away an afternoon.

Waianapanapa State Park. For more detailed information on Hana's sights, see the tour on p 41.

Continue past Hana on Hwy. 31 to Ulupalakua. The drive should take about an hour.

9 **Tedeschi Vineyards.** Get a picnic lunch before you leave Hana and drive the "backside" around Maui past Kaupo to the winery. After sampling a few of Maui's wines, select a bottle and have your picnic lunch on the grounds of the old estate. See p 41.

Head north on Hwy. 37, to a right on Hwy. 377 for about a quarter of a mile. Once you've rounded the bend, take a quick right up Waipoli Rd.

10 **Alii Kula Lavender.** In the upcountry Kula region, stop at this lavender farm to pick up lavender bubble bath and a lavender candle. Plan to spend your final night soaking in a romantic hot bath in Maui's Upcountry. *1100 Waipoli Rd. Kula (☎ 808/878-3004; www.aliikula lavender.com).*

Retrace your steps to Hwy. 37, take a right at the light on Makawao Rd., and at the stop sign in Makawao town go left down Baldwin Ave. to the end.

⓫ **Paia.** On your last day, drive to Paia and have breakfast at my favorite cafe, **Moana Bakery & Café** (p 129). Afterwards poke around the shops in this tiny town. See chapter 9.

Turn right on Hwy. 36.

⓬ **Hookipa.** Here you can watch the surfers and windsurfers as you feel the warm wind caress your face. This is a great spot for a photo op with that glorious ocean as a backdrop. See p 78.

Windsurfers on Hookipa.

Getting Maui'd

Maui is a great place for a wedding. Not only does the entire island exude romance and natural beauty, but after the ceremony, you're only a few steps away from the perfect honeymoon.

Dozens of companies can help you organize an unforgettable wedding. The easiest option is to let someone at the resort or hotel where you'll be staying handle it. Most Maui resorts and hotels have wedding coordinators who can plan everything from a simple (relatively) low-cost wedding to an extravaganza that people will talk about for years. Remember that resorts can be pricey—be frank with your wedding coordinator if you want to keep costs down.

You can also plan your own island wedding, even from afar, without spending a fortune. For a marriage license, contact the **Marriage License Office,** State Department of Health Building, 54 S. High St., Wailuku, HI 96793 (☎ 808/984-8210; www.state.hi.us/doh/records/vr_marri.html), open Monday through Friday from 8am to 4pm. The staff will mail you a brochure called *Getting Married* and direct you to the marriage-licensing agent closest to where you'll be staying on Maui. Once on Maui the prospective bride and groom must go together to the marriage-licensing agent to get a license. A license costs $60 and is good for 30 days.

The Wailea Resort's wedding chapel.

The Best Special-Interest Tours

Relax & Rejuvenate on Maui

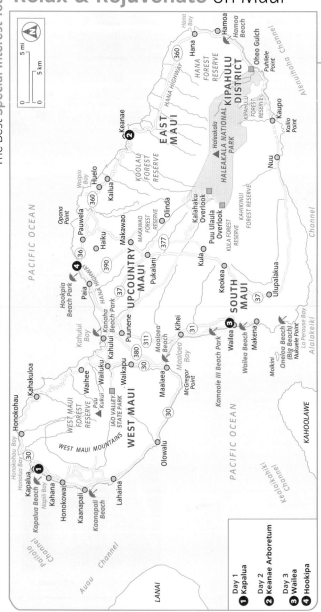

Day 1
1 Kapalua

Day 2
2 Keanae Arboretum

Day 3
3 Wailea
4 Hookipa

Maui's beautiful weather, unspoiled beaches, lush tropical vegetation, and invigorating tradewinds are just the recipe to soothe your body, mind, and spirit. Below are my favorite ways to relax over a 3-day weekend. START: Kapalua. Trip length: 3 days and 195 miles (314km)

1 Kapalua. Start the day off by booking a massage on the beach at the **Ritz-Carlton Kapalua** (p 117). The spa itself is welcoming and wonderful, but I love the smell of salt in the air and feeling the wind gently caressing my hair while experiencing a true Hawaiian massage. Grab a picnic lunch at the **Honolua Store** (p 140) and walk down to **D. T. Fleming Beach** (p 78) and plan to spend the afternoon just reading a good book or floating in the warm, tropical waters. For a soothing, relaxing dinner, try the **Pineapple Grill Kapalua** (p 129)

Head south on Hwy. 30 and go left on Hwy. 380. Go right on Hwy. 30, which becomes Hwy. 360. The rainforest is after MM 16, just past the Keanae YMCA Camp and before the turn off to the Keanae Peninsula. Allow 2 to 3 hours for the 80-mile (128.8km) trip.

2 Keanae Arboretum. This easy 2-mile (3.2km) stroll through the rainforest is a wonderful way to relax and commune with nature. (Excepting mosquitoes and rain—

bring repellant and rain gear to ward them off.) I'd allow at least 2 hours here, longer if you bring your swim suit and plunge into my favorite swimming hole near the end of the trail. Park at the Keanae Arboretum and pass through the turnstile. You start off on a flat trail where you can look around at the plants which have been introduced to Hawaii (all with identification tags). At the end of this section is a taro patch, with a half dozen different varieties of this staple crop. Next, a 1-mile (1.6km) trail takes you into a lush Hawaiian rainforest. Stop and smell the fragrances of this tropical jungle; listen to the sounds of the birds and the nearby stream. You can follow the trail as it crisscrosses the stream through the forest, but I prefer to cool off at the pond, just to the left of the first stream crossing. Plan to spend the night in Hana (about 40 minutes down the highway) at the **Hotel Hana-Maui** (see p 115).

Head south on Hwy. 31, which becomes Hwy. 37 after Ulupalakua. Continue on Hwy. 37 at Pukalani. Go left on Hwy. 36, left

A Healthy Vacation

Plan your Maui trip in early September to coincide with the **LifeFest Kapalua** (☎ 866/669-2440; www.lifefestmaui.com), a 3-day health-and-wellness event, held at the Kapalua Resort. The event features lectures and panel presentations by leaders in the health and wellness field, plus ocean sporting events, fitness activities, a health and wellness expo, and sumptuous gala dinners.

Relax, Breathe Deep & Say Sp-Ahh

Hawaii's spas are airy, open facilities that embrace the tropics. Here are your best options on Maui:

- **Spa Grande at the Grand Wailea Resort** (☎ 800/888-6100 or 808/875-1234; www.grandwailea.com): This is Hawaii's biggest spa, combining the finest Eastern traditions (a full Japanese-style traditional bath and various exotic treatments from India), and the lure of the islands (tropical foliage, ancient Hawaiian treatments, and island products). Everything from a top fitness center to a menu of classes.
- **Spa Kea Lani at The Fairmont Kea Lani Maui** (☎ 800/659-4100 or 808/875-4100; www.fairmont.com/kealani): This intimate, Art Deco boutique spa is the place for personal, private attention. The fitness center next door is open 24 hours (a rarity in Hawaiian resorts) with a personal trainer on duty some 14 hours a day.
- **Spa Moana at the Hyatt Regency Maui Resort & Spa** (☎ 800/233-1234 or 808/661-1234; www.maui.hyatt.com): The facility offers an open-air exercise lanai, wet-treatment rooms, massage rooms, a relaxation lounge, sauna and steam rooms, a Roman pool illuminated by overhead skylights, and a duet treatment suite for couples.

Enjoying a massage at The Fairmont.

- **Spa at Ritz-Carlton Kapalua** (☎ 800/262-8440 or 808/669-6200; www.ritzcarlton.com): Book a massage on the beach. The spa itself is welcoming and wonderful.
- **The Spa at the Four Seasons Resort Maui at Wailea** (☎ 800/334-MAUI [6284] or 808/874-8000; www.fourseasons.com/maui): Imagine the sounds of the waves rolling on Wailea Beach as you are soothingly massaged in the privacy of your cabana, tucked into the beachside foliage. This is the place to come to be absolutely spoiled.

A painted eucalyptus tree with a philo-dendron leaf at the Keanae Arboretum.

on Hansen Rd., left on Hwy. 311, and left again on Hwy. 31. When 31 ends, take a right onto Wailea Iki Dr. Then go left on Wailea Alanui Dr. Allow 2 to 3 hours for the 65-mile (104.6km) trip.

❸ Wailea. This is the holy land of spas. I'd book one of the following: a Seashell Massage (using seashells in combination with the Hawaiian lomi lomi massage for relief to tense muscles, sore joints, and stressed emotions) at the **Spa Grande at the Grand Wailea Resort;** the Signature Treatment (four diverse techniques, including a peppermint scrub, warm herbal wrap, massage medley, finishing with a soothing scalp treatment) at **The Spa at the Four Seasons Resort Maui;** or the Blissful Spa Experience (gotu kola, noni, and kava kava scrub, then an aroma tropical bath, followed by a Hawaiian lomi lomi massage) at the

Spa Kea Lani at The Fairmont Kea Lani Maui. See box on p 36 for details. After your treatment, lunch at **Longhi's** (p 128).

From Wailea take Hwy. 31 north, go right on Hwy. 311 and right again on Hwy. 36 to Hookipa. Allow 40 to 45 minutes driving time.

❹ Hookipa. In the afternoon sit on the bluff overlooking this windsurfing beach (p 78) and watch the colorful sailboarders lift into the air and twirl like butterflies. At sunset, simply go next door for a fresh fish dinner at **Mama's Fish House** (p 128).

Relaxing in a hammock on Wailea beach.

Maui's Farmlands

Day 1
① Hawaiian Pineapple Plantation
② Maui Tropical Plantation

Day 2
③ Surfing Goat Dairy
④ Alii Kai Lavender
⑤ Sunrise Protea

Day 3
⑥ Tedeschi Vineyards
⑦ Kahanu Garden

When people think of Maui, flowers and leis often come to mind, but Maui's fertile soil grows lush fields of everything from tropical fruit and exotic flowers to breadfruit and lavender. The island even produces goat cheese and wine. Below are my favorite tours of Maui's bounty. START: **Kapalua**. Trip length: 3 days and 116 miles (186.8km)

① Hawaiian Pineapple Plantation. Start with Hawaii's king of fruits by taking the 2-hour Hawaiian Pineapple Plantation Tour led by experienced plantation workers, who guide you through a pineapple field in the midst of a harvest. Their colorful commentary weaves the pineapple's history into facts about its growing and harvesting cycles. *The Kapalua Villas Reception Center, across from the Honolua Store, Office Rd., Kapalua (☎ 808/669-8088; www.kapaluamaui.com/activities/adventure/pineapple.html).*

A luscious Maui pineapple.

Travel south on Hwy. 30 for 27 miles (43.5km). Allow about 40 to 45 minutes.

② kids Maui Tropical Plantation. The Maui Tropical Plantation

Tour is a 45- to 60-minute narrated tram tour of this 60-acre working plantation that produces tropical fruits and flowers (papaya, guava, mango, macadamia nuts, coffee, avocado, bananas, sugar cane, star fruit, and more). Don't forget to stop by the store and pick up your favorite fruit. *Between MM 2 and 3, on Hwy. 30, Waikapu (☎ 800/451-6805; www. mauitropicalplantation.com).*

Head north on Hwy. 30, go right at the light on Main St. and continue through Wailuku and Kahului. Continue on Hwy. 36, take a right on Pulehu Rd., and veer left on Omaopio Rd., which is about a mile down on the right. Allow 30 to 40 minutes.

Maui's Farmers' Market

If you want the freshest Maui fruits, flowers, and produce (at budget prices), show up at the farmers' market closest to where you're staying.

Kahului has four farmers' markets to choose from: Every Tuesday and Friday, from 7am to 3pm at the **Queen Ka'ahumanu Center;** on Tuesday, Wednesday, and Friday, from 8am to 5pm at the **Maui Mall Shopping Center;** on Wednesday from 6am to 1pm at the **Kahului Shopping Center;** and my personal favorite, on Friday, from noon to 6pm, at the **Maui Community College.**

If you are staying in the **Kihei** area, on Monday, Wednesday, and Friday, from 1 to 5pm, there's a farmer's market at the **Suda Store.**

Wow! Look at the Size of that Fish

Enormous fish swim around the island of Maui. The largest, a Pacific blue marlin caught in Maui waters, tipped the scale at 1,200 pounds and was 15-feet long. If you want to see what Hawaii's big game fish look like, wander down to the docks at Lahaina or Maalaea either just after noon or around 5pm when the sport-fishing boats return with their catch. At the end of October, the island's largest fishing tournament takes place in Lahaina, the **Lahaina Jackpot Fishing Tournament.** Some 75 teams compete to haul in the "big one." During the event, nightly fish weigh-ins take place at the Lahaina Harbor starting at 4pm. For more information contact the **Lahaina Yacht Club,** 835 Front St., Lahaina (☎ 808/661-0191; www.lahaina yachtclub.org).

Men posing with marlins.

❸ kids Surfing Goat Dairy. In Kula, just beyond the sugar-cane fields and on the slopes of Haleakala, lies this dairy, where some 140 dairy goats blissfully graze the 42 acres and contribute the milk for the 24 different cheeses, which are made every day. Choose from the 2-hour **Grand Dairy Tour,** where you can learn how to milk a goat, make cheese, and sample the different varieties; or drop by for the 20-minute casual dairy tour. *3651 Omaopio Rd., Kula (☎ 808/878-2870; www.surfinggoatdairy.com)*

Continue up Omaopio Rd. to Hwy. 37 and turn right. At your second left after Rice Park, turn on Hwy. 377, drive about ¼ mile, rounding a bend and taking a quick right up Waipoli Rd. Allow 20 to 30 minutes.

Head for lunch at **❹ Alii Kai Lavender,** where a variety of terrific tours take you to see the various varieties of lavender that bloom year-round. You can choose either the 50-minute **Walking Tour,** which

Protea.

Breadfruit.

explores the grounds; the **Lavender Garden Tea Tour,** a tea party featuring lavender herb tea with a lavender scone and a garden and studio tour; or my favorite, the **Lavender Garden Culinary Tour,** which includes lunch and a cooking demonstration that incorporates their lavender products. *1100 Waipoli Rd., Kula (☎ 808/878-3004; www.aliikula lavender.com).*

Go right on Hwy. 377 to Hwy. 378. Allow about 15 minutes.

5 Sunrise Protea. After lunch, you'll have plenty of time to see Maui's most unusual flower, the other-worldly protea, which is actually native to South Africa. On Haleakala's rich volcanic slopes, Sunrise Protea offers a walk-through garden tour, a gift shop, friendly service, and a larger-than-usual selection of these exotic flowers. If you can swing it, go on a Tuesday or a Friday, when the just-cut flowers come in from the fields. *Haleakala Hwy., Kula (☎ 800/222-2797; www.sunriseprotea.com)*

From Kula take Hwy. 378 to Hwy. 377, then make a left turn on Hwy. 37. The winery is another 12 miles (19.3km) down the road. Allow 30 to 45 minutes.

6 Tedeschi Vineyards. Plan to arrive in time for the 10:30am tour (the other one is at 1:30pm) of the grounds and wine-producing operation at Maui's only winery. Not only will you get to see the historic grounds, including the tasting room, which was the guest cottage built for King Kalakaua in 1874, but you'll also learn about the six different varietals grown on the slopes of Haleakala. *Ulupalakua. ☎ 877/878-6058. www.mauiwine.com. Tasting room open daily 9am–5pm.*

Take 31 east to Hana. Just before MM 31, turn down Ulaino Rd. toward the ocean. Allow about an hour's driving time.

7 Kahanu Garden. The world's largest collection of breadfruit trees—a staple food crop for Pacific islanders—can be found here. The garden has some 130 distinct varieties gathered from 20 tropical island groups. Also here is the **Canoe Garden,** which assembles all the useful plants that the early Polynesian settlers brought to Hawaii: sugar cane, banana, sweet potato, taro, turmeric, and paper mulberry (used to make kapa cloth). *Ulaino Rd (turn towards the ocean at MM 31 off the Hana Hwy.) ☎ 808/248-8912; www.ntbg.org/gardens/kahanu.html*

Maui's History & Culture

Kapalua

Area of
map below

PACIFIC OCEAN

Wailuku   Kahului

WEST
MAUI

Lahaina

UPCOUNTRY
MAUI

EAST
MAUI

Hana

M A U I

HALEAKALA
NATIONAL
PARK

KIPAHULU
DISTRICT

Wailea

Ulupalakua

SOUTH
MAUI

PACIFIC OCEAN

Auau Channel

Kealoikahiki
Channel

Wailuku

0   1/2 mi

0   0.5 km

Kuhio
Onaha Pl

Kahekili Hwy.

E. Main St.

Maui Arts &
Culture Center

Kahului
Bay

Pilhana Rd.

Iao Stream

Lihliho

Kahului
Harbor

WAILUKU

KEOPUOLANI
PARK

KAHULUI
HARBOR
PARK

Kanaloa Ave.

Kahului Bech Rd.

N. Market St.

Main St.

War Memorial
Park

Mokuhau Rd.

W. Vineyard St.

W. Main St.

S. Church St.

Waiale Dr.

S. High St.

Kaahumanu Ave.

KAHULUI

Wakea Ave.

MAUI
MEMORIAL
PARK

Papa Ave.

Maui Pineapple
Company

Days 1 & 2	Day 2	Day 3
① Lahaina	② Whale Center of the Pacific	⑨ Hana
	③ Kapalua	
	④ Kahekili Highway (Hwy. 340)	Day 4
	④A Kahakuloa	⑩ Ulupalakua Ranch
	④B Wailuku	⑪ Makawao
	(Halekii & Pihanakalani Heiau)	⑫ Paia
	⑤ Maui Bake Shop	
	⑥ Bailey House Museum	
	⑦ Iao Valley State Park	
	⑧ Puunene	

It is possible to walk back in time on Maui, back to the ancient Hawaiians who first came to the island, to the missionaries and whalers who arrived in the 1800s, to the plantation workers and cowboys of the 1900s, and most recently, to the hippies of the 1960s and 1970s. Plan to spend your first night in West Maui, your second night in Wailuku, and your third in Hana. START: Lahaina. Trip Length: 4 days and 190 miles (305.9km)

1 **Lahaina.** This old town, whose name translates as "merciless sun," has archeological evidence dating back to A.D. 700. If you've just arrived, a terrific way to dip your toes into Maui culture is at the **Old Lahaina Luau** (see p 150). The next morning you can start your first full day in Maui with a hearty breakfast, followed by a hands-on cultural experience at **Ho'omana'o** (p 44). Head over to the **Baldwin Home Museum** to begin the Lahaina tour (p 50), which covers the days of the whalers and missionaries and their effect on Lahaina.

Take Hwy. 30 north to Kaanapali, a 5-minute drive.

2 **Whale Center of the Pacific.** For more on the whalers, stop by Whalers Village in Kaanapali, at this museum celebrating the "Golden Era of Whaling" (1825–1860). Harpoons and scrimshaw are on display and the museum has even re-created the

cramped quarters of a whaler's seagoing vessel. ⏱ *30 min. Whalers Village, 2435 Kaanapali Pkwy., Kaanapali. (☎ 808/661-5992. www.whalersvillage.com. Daily 9:30am–10pm. Free admission.*

Continue north on Hwy. 30 to Kapalua, a 10- to 15-minute drive.

3 **Kapalua.** To go back even farther in time, drive out to Kapalua ("two borders") where on the hill, on the ocean side of the Ritz-Carlton Kapalua, the burial sites of hundreds of ancient Hawaiians were discovered in the sand. The hotel, which was under construction at the time of the discovery, was moved inland to avoid disturbing the graves. You'll find a plaque here detailing their history.

Continue north, past Kapalua, on Hwy. 30 (which becomes Hwy. 340, then Hwy. 330, and then N. Market St.). Go left on Mills St., left again on Lower Main St., and follow this street until it ends at Hwy. 340, and make another left.

Baldwin Home Museum.

Kahakuloa Village.

Go left again on Kuhio St. and then take your first left on Hea Pl., following it to the end. Allow 45 minutes to an hour to reach Wailuku.

④ Kahekili Highway (Hwy. 340). Along this highway (named for the great chief Kahekili, who built houses from the skulls of his enemies), nestled in a crevice between two steep hills, is the picturesque village of **④A Kahakuloa** ("the tall hau tree"), with a dozen weather-worn houses, a church with a red-tile roof, and vivid green taro patches. Life here has not changed much during the past few decades. Continue into **④B Wailuku** to see two ancient sites: **Halekii** and **Pihanakalani Heiau**, built in 1240

from stones carried up from the Iao Stream below. Chief Kahekili lived here. After the bloody battle at Iao Stream, Kamehameha I (the king who united the Hawaiian Islands) reportedly came to the temple here to pay homage to the war god, Ku, with a human sacrifice. Halekii ("House of Images") has stone walls and a flat grassy top, whereas Pihanakalani ("gathering place of supernatural beings") is a pyramid-shaped mound of stones. If you sit quietly nearby (never walk on any *heiau*—it's considered disrespectful), you'll see that the view alone explains why this spot was chosen.

⑤ Maui Bake Shop. Sure, you can buy a great smelling loaf of bread, baked in one of Maui's oldest brick ovens (dating to 1935), or one of the sumptuous fresh-fruit gâteaux, puff pastries, or dozens of other baked goods, but I recommend holding out for the white-chocolate macadamia-nut cheesecake. *2092 Vineyard St. (at N. Church St.), Wailuku.* ☎ *808/242-0064. $.*

Retrace your steps and turn left at N. Market St. Go right on Vineyard St., and left on High St. At the

A Feast of Memories

Ho'omana'o (to remember), a 3-hour feast and immersion into ancient Hawaii, is a must for people interested in Hawaiian culture. The feast begins with a breakfast buffet ranging from island stuffed French toast to Kalua pork with lomi salmon to *haupia* (coconut) oatmeal, accompanied by Hula dancers and chanters. Then the fun begins, with active audience participation in three aspects of Hawaii: hula, warfare, and ancient life. Located at 1251 Front St., Lahaina (☎ **800/248-5828;** www.oldlahainaluau.com). Hours are Wed and Fri, 8:30 to 11:30am. The cost is $69 for adults and $49 for children 12 and under.

light, turn right on Main St.; Bailey House Museum is on the left.

6 ★★ Bailey House Museum.

Moving forward both literally and historically, the next stop is the 1833 home of missionary and sugar planter Edward Bailey, containing one of my favorite treasure troves of Hawaiiana, with everything from scary temple images, dog-tooth necklaces, and a rare lei made of tree-snail shells, to latter-day relics like Duke Kahanamoku's 1919 redwood surfboard. ⏲ 30–45 min. 2375-A Main St. ☎ 808/244-3326. www.mauimuseum.org. Admission $5 adults, $4 seniors, $1 children 7–12, free for children 6 and under. Mon–Sat 10am–4pm.

Continue up Main St., which becomes Iao Valley Rd., to the end.

7 Iao Valley State Park. It's

hard to imagine that peaceful **Iao Stream** was the site of one of Maui's worst battles. In 1790 King Kamehameha the Great and his men fought at Iao Valley to gain control of Maui. When the battle ended, so many bodies blocked the stream that the battle site was named Kepaniwai, or "damming of the waters." The park and stream get their names from the Iao Needle, a phallic rock that juts an impressive 2,250 feet above sea level. Iao in Hawaiian means "supreme light."

Retrace your steps to Main St. and continue straight through Wailuku and Kahului. Turn right at the light on to S. Puunene Ave, and continue until Hansen Rd. in Puunene.

8 Puunene. In the middle of the

central Maui plains, the town of Puunene ("Goose Hill") has almost disappeared. Once a thriving sugar-plantation town with hundreds of homes, a school, a shopping area, and a community center, today Puunene is little more than a sugar

mill, a post office, and the **Alexander & Baldwin Sugar Museum,** Puunene Ave./Hwy. 350 and Hansen Rd. (☎ 808/871-8058; www.sugar museum.com). This former sugar-mill superintendent's home has been converted into a museum that tells the story of sugar in Hawaii, from how sugar is grown, harvested, and milled, to how Samuel Alexander and Henry Baldwin (founders of Maui's largest sugar plantation, HC&S) managed to acquire huge chunks of land from the Kingdom of Hawaii, then ruthlessly fought to gain access to water on the other side of the island, making sugar cane an economically viable crop. A great place to spend the night is the historic **Old Wailuku Inn at Ulupono** (p 117), a 1924 former plantation manager's home that's been lovingly restored.

Take Kaahumanu Ave., which becomes Hwy. 36. Hwy. 36 then becomes Hwy. 360 to Hana. Allow 2 to 3 hours.

9 Hana. The Hana coast is rich in

Hawaiian history and the scene of many turning points in Hawaiian culture. The ancient chants tell of rulers like 15th-century Piilani, who united the island of Maui and built fishponds and

Bailey House Museum sign.

46

irrigation fields, paved roads, and constructed the massive **Piilanihale Heiau** (temple), which still stands today. It was Piilani's sons and grandson who finished the *heiau* and built the first road to Hana from West Maui, not only along the coast, but also up the Kaupo Gap and through the Haleakala Crater. Once in Hana, make sure to stop at the **Hana Cultural Center and Museum** (p 72 ❸), with the **Kauhala O Hana,** composed of four traditional Hawaiian *hale* (houses) for living, meeting, cooking, and canoe building or canoe storage. In Hana Bay lies a 386-foot (115.8m), red-faced cinder cone, **Kauiki Hill,** the scene of numerous fierce battles in ancient Hawaii and the birthplace of Queen Kaahumanu in 1768.

Continue on Hwy. 31 past Hana to Ulupalakua. The drive takes about an hour.

❿ **Ulupalakua Ranch.** High on the slopes of Haleakala, Ulupalakua ("breadfruit ripening") tells Maui's agricultural history, starting with sugar in 1845 when King Kamehameha III leased 2,000 acres (800 hectares) of what was then called Honua'ula ("red land"). Eleven years later, Captain James Makee added 1,600 head of livestock to the ranch. In 1874 King David Kalakaua, the Merrie Monarch, visited the ranch so often a cottage was built for him on

A view of Upcountry Maui.

the property, which still exists today as the site of the **Tedeschi Vineyards'** (p 41) tasting room. In 1883 the last sugar crop was processed at the Ulupalakua Mill and the area became a working cattle ranch. After changing hands several times over the next 8 decades, current owner C. Pardee Erdman purchased the property in 1963 and named it Ulupalakua Ranch.

Drive north on Hwy. 37 and go right at the light on Makawao Ave. for approximately 30 minutes.

⓫ **Makawao**. This cowboy town dates back to 1888 when the Haleakala Ranch was founded to control the cattle introduced in Hawaii in 1793. Horses didn't arrive on Maui until sea captain Richard Cleveland offered some as a gift to King Kamehameha the Great in 1803. Seventeen years later the *"pipi'ahiu"* (wild cattle) population had exploded and the cattle were being hunted upcountry. Today cowboys still ride their horses into Makawao ("forest beginning") and tie up at the hitching posts along Baldwin Ave.

Drive down Baldwin Ave until the end. Allow 15- to 20-minutes driving time.

⓬ **Paia.** Once a thriving sugar-mill town, Paia ("noisy") became the most important community along Maui's North Shore during the 1880s when the Alexander and Baldwin Company built the first sugar mill on the island just outside of town. The mill is still here, but the population shifted to Kahului in the 1950s when subdivisions opened there, leaving Paia to shrivel up and die. But the town has proved remarkably adaptable, becoming a popular hippie hangout in the 1960s and 1970s (some of the shops retain a bit of residual counterculture from those days) and developing an international reputation as a windsurfing mecca in the 1980s. ●

4 The Best Regional & Town Tours

West Maui

1 Olowalu
2 Lahaina
3 Kaanapali
4 Kapalua

This is the fabled Maui you see on postcards: Jagged peaks, green valleys, crystal clear water, and sandy beaches. The stretch of coastline from Kapalua to the historic port of Lahaina is the island's busiest resort area (with South Maui a close second). Expect a few mainland-style traffic jams. START: **Olowalu**. Trip length: 17 miles (27.4km)

1 **kids Olowalu.** Most visitors drive right past this tiny hamlet, 5 miles (8km) south of Lahaina. If you blink you'll miss the general store and Chez Paul Restaurant (p 26). Olowalu ("many hills") was the scene of the 1790 massacre, when the Hawaiians stole a skiff from the USS *Eleanora*, and the captain of the ship retaliated by mowing them down with his cannons, killing 100 people and wounding many others. Stop at **Mile Marker (MM) 14,** for one of my favorite snorkeling spots—over a turtle-cleaning station about 150 to 225 feet (45–67.5m) out from

shore—to see turtles lining up to have cleaner wrasses (small fish) pick parasites off their shells. Take at least 30 minutes to watch the turtles.

Take Hwy. 30 north 7 miles (11.3km).

Travel Tip

I've used the highway number, not the name of the highway, when detailing how to get around on Maui. The abbreviation MM stands for "mile marker." For more information, see "Maui Driving Tips" on p 12.

2 ★★★ **kids Lahaina.** Plan a minimum of a half day in Lahaina. See p 27.

Take Hwy. 30 3 miles (4.8km) north of Lahaina.

3 Kaanapali. Hawaii's first master-planned resort consists of pricey mid-rise hotels, lining nearly 3 miles (4.8km) of gold-sand beach. Golf greens wrap around the slope between beachfront and hillside properties. Inside Kaanapali Resort, turn toward the ocean from Hwy. 30 on Kaanapali Pkwy to reach **Whalers Village,** a seaside mall (for information on the stores here, see p 43), that has adopted the whale as its mascot. You can't miss the huge (almost life-size) metal sculpture of a mother whale and two nursing calves that greets you. The reason to stop here is the tiny museum inside Whalers Village, **kids Whale Center of the Pacific** (p 43, which celebrates the "Golden Era of Whaling" from 1825 to 1860. It's small, but packed with wonderful displays from harpoons to

scrimshaw; my favorite exhibit is the re-created cramped quarters of a whaler's seagoing vessel (it will make you stop complaining about the size of your hotel room!). Self-guided audio tours and short videos are available throughout the day.

Continue north on Hwy. 30 for 7 miles (11.3km).

4 ★ **Kapalua.** As you continue on Hwy. 30, the vista opens up to fields of silver-green pineapple and manicured golf fairways. Turn down Office Road, a country lane bordered by Pacific pines marching toward the sea. This is the exclusive domain of the luxurious **Ritz-Carlton Kapalua** (p 117), located next to two bays that are marine-life preserves (with fabulous surfing in winter). The resort has an art school, a golf school, three golf courses (p 93), historic features, a collection of swanky condos and homes, and wide-open spaces that include a rainforest preserve—all open to the general public. Pack a picnic lunch and spend a day here.

Whale skeleton at Whaler's Village.

Lahaina

1. Baldwin Home Museum
2. Pioneer Inn
3. Banyan Tree
4. Courthouse
5. Maui Swiss Café
6. Maluuluulele Park
7. Wainee Church and Cemetery
8. Hongwanji Mission
9. Old Prison
10. Buddhist Church
11. Luakini Street
12. Maui Sunrise Café
13. Wo Hing Temple
14. Lahaina Jodo Mission

Between the West Maui Mountains and the deep azure ocean offshore, Lahaina stands out as one of the few places in Hawaii that has managed to preserve its 19th-century heritage while still accommodating 21st-century guests. It has been the royal capital of Hawaii, the main center of the whaling industry, the place where missionaries tried to save the Hawaiians, the home of a sugar plantation, and today, one of the most popular towns in Maui for visitors to explore. START: **Baldwin Home Museum on Front St. Trip length: 2 miles (3.2km)**

---

1 Baldwin Home Museum.

Start your journey back into the 19th century by stepping inside this coral and rock structure, the oldest house in Lahaina, and imagining what it must have been like to live here as a foreigner in 1834 when Rev. Dwight Baldwin, a doctor with the American missionaries, built it. Next door is the **Masters' Reading Room**, Maui's oldest building. ⏱ 30

min. 120 Dickenson St. (at Front St.). ☎ 808/661-3262; www.lahaina restoration.org. Admission $3 adults, $2 seniors, $5 families. Daily 10am–4:30pm.

2 Pioneer Inn.
Wander into Lahaina's first hotel, which looks pretty much the way it did when it was built in 1901. If the walls of this old building could talk, they would be singing about some pretty wild

parties at the turn of the 20th century. George Freeland, of the Royal Canadian Mounted Police, tracked a criminal to Lahaina and then fell in love with the town, building this hotel, which is still open for business. You can also get a cold drink at the old bar on the south side of the hotel and watch the goings-on at the harbor. 🕐 *30 min. if you stop for a drink. 658 Wharf St. ☎ 808/ 661-3636; www.pioneerinnmaui. com.*

3 kids **Banyan Tree.** This is every kid's dream—a tree made for climbing. Of all the banyan trees in Hawaii, this is the largest, so big that you can't get it in your camera's viewfinder. It was only 8-feet (2.4m) tall when it was planted in 1873 by Maui sheriff William O. Smith to mark the 50th anniversary of Lahaina's first Christian mission. Now it's more than 50 feet tall, has 12 major trunks, and shades ⅔ of an acre in Courthouse Square. You can sit down in the shade and people-watch for a few minutes. 🕐 *15 min. if you have kids. At the Courthouse Building, 649 Wharf St.*

4 **Courthouse.** This building served not only as a courthouse, but also as a custom house, post office, tax collector's office, and government offices. Although it looks stuffy on the outside, be sure and go up to the second floor to visit the **Lahaina Heritage Museum,** which has exhibits on the history and culture of Lahaina. My favorite is the 3-dimensional relief map of Maui, a bird's eye view of the island's topography. 🕐 *20 min. 648 Wharf St., Lahaina. ☎ 808/661-1959; www.visitlahaina.com. Free admission. Daily 9am–5pm.*

5 **Maui Swiss Café.** This is a great place for tropical smoothies, strong espresso, and affordable snacks. You can sit in the somewhat funky garden area, or (my preference) get your drink to go and wander over to the seawall to watch the surfers. *640 Front St. ☎ 808/661-6776. $.*

6 **Maluuluulele Park.** Though not much to look at now, this park and ball field was once a sacred stop for Hawaiians. It used to be a village, Mokuhinia, with a revered pond that was the home of a *moo* (a spirit in the form of a lizard), which the royal family honored as their personal guardian spirit. I recommend this stop because it can help visitors appreciate how the Hawaiians feel about the destruction of their culture and religion. (Imagine the Statue of Liberty being torn down and replaced with a dusty ball park.) 🕐 *5–10 min. Front/Shaw sts.*

Pioneer Inn.

7 Wainee Church and Cemetery. The first stone church in Hawaii (1828–32) was built here. The current church has been standing since 1953. Be sure to walk around to the back of the church: The row of palm trees on the ocean side includes some of the oldest palm trees in Lahaina. Next door is the first Christian cemetery in Hawaii, the Waihee Cemetery, established in 1823. It tells a fascinating story of old Hawaii, with graves of Hawaiian chiefs, commoners, missionaries, and their families (infant mortality was high then), and sailors. ⏱ *10–15 min. Wainee/Shaw sts.*

8 Hongwanji Mission. The temple was originally built in 1910 by members of Lahaina's Buddhist sect. The current building was constructed in 1927, housing a temple and a language school. Although the church is not always open, the reverend who lives next door takes the time to talk to visitors and will give a tour of the church to those who are interested. ⏱ *5 min., longer if you get a tour inside. Wainee/Luakini sts.*

9 Old Prison. The Hawaiians called the prison Hale Paahao

A gravestone in Waimee Cemetery.

("stuck in irons house"). Sailors who refused to return to their boats at sunset were sent here. If the doors are open, wander inside and see the brick-walled area surrounding the center courtyard. Unfortunately it seems to be closed most days. ⏱ *5 min. Wainee/Prison sts.*

10 Buddhist Church. Most likely it will be closed, but this green wooden Shingon Buddhist temple is typical of the myriad Buddhist churches that sprang up all over the island when the Japanese laborers were brought to work in the sugar-cane fields. ⏱ *2 min. Luakini/Hale sts.*

11 Luakini Street. Sometimes to experience Hawaii you have to feel with your heart, and not "look" with your eyes. This is one of those places. "Luakini" translates as a *heiau* (temple) where the ruling chiefs prayed and where human sacrifices were made. This street received its unforgettable name after serving as the route for the funeral procession of Princess Harriet Nahienaena, sister of kings Kamehameha II and III. The princess was a victim of the rapid changes in Hawaiian culture. A convert to Protestantism, she fell in love with her brother at an early age. Just 20 years earlier, their relationship would have been nurtured in order to preserve the purity of the royal bloodlines. The missionaries, however, frowned on a brother and sister marrying. In August 1836 the couple had a son, who lived only a few short hours. Nahienaena never recovered and died in December of that same year. The route of her funeral procession through the breadfruit and koa trees to the cemetery became known as Luakini, in reference to the gods "sacrificing" the beloved princess. Stop on this street in the shade of one of the big breadfruit trees, and try to imagine the sorrow and fear of a population

Wo Hing Temple.

in transition. The old ways were dying—and the new ways were foreign and frightening.

🕐 **Maui Sunrise Café.** Take a break at this tiny cafe on Front Street, next door to the library. Grab a cup of java and one of their delicious baked goods and relax in the patio garden out back. *693A Front St., Lahaina.* ☎ *808/661-8558. $.*

🔞 **Wo Hing Temple.** I love this temple; it's so well preserved that you'd swear they're just getting ready to hold a Saturday social. The Chinese were among the various immigrants brought to Hawaii to work in the sugar-cane fields. In 1909 several Chinese workers formed the Wo Hing society, a chapter of the Chee Kun Tong society, which dates from the 17th century. In 1912 they built this social hall for the Chinese community. Completely restored, the Wo Hing Temple contains displays and artifacts on the history of the Chinese in Lahaina. Be sure to wander next door to the cookhouse and watch the old movies of Hawaii taken by Thomas Edison in 1898 and 1903. 🕐 *20 min. Front St. (between Wahie Lane and Papalaua St.).* ☎ *808/661-3262.*

Admission by donation. Daily 10am–4pm.

🔞 **Lahaina Jodo Mission.** The first thing you'll see when you enter the grounds is the Great Buddha statue (some 12 ft. high and weighing 3½ tons). Seeing the Buddha is worth the trip alone. This site was sacred to the Hawaiians who called it Puunoa Point, meaning "the hill freed from taboo." Once a small village named *Mala* (garden), this peaceful place became a haven for Japanese immigrants. In 1968, on the 100th anniversary of the Japanese arrival in Hawaii, the giant Buddha statue was brought here from Japan. 🕐 *10–15 min. 12 Ala Moana St. (off Front St., near the Mala Wharf).* ☎ *808/661-4304. Free admission. Daily during daylight hours.*

Great Buddha statue.

South Maui

1 Ahihi-Kinau
2 Longhi's
3 Makena
4 Wailea
5 Joy's Place
6 Kihei
7 Maui Ocean Center
8 The Waterfront at Maalaea

To really see the hottest, sunniest, driest coastline on Maui—Arizona by the sea—you have to get out of your car and walk, paddle along the ocean in a kayak, or get in the water. You cannot experience this oceanside area merely by looking out the window as you drive by. On former scrubland from Maalaea to Makena, where cacti once grew wild and cows grazed, are now four distinct areas—Maalaea, Kihei, Wailea, and Makena—and a surprising amount of traffic. START: **Ahini-Kinau Natural Area and preserve. Trip Length: 20 miles (32.2km), but allow a full day to truly experience Maui's southern shore**

Travel Tip

Before you start this tour, pack a swimsuit, towels, good hiking shoes, sunscreen, a hat, plenty of water and (depending on what you want to do) maybe rent snorkel gear and/or a kayak (see chapter 6 for rental recommendations). Be sure to get up early to avoid the hot sun; you'll want to start off before 7am in the winter and 6am in the summer for the most comfortable temperatures.

Drive south on Makena Rd., past Puu Olai to Ahihi Bay, where the road turns to gravel. Go another 2 miles (3.2km) along the coast to La Pérouse Bay.

A sunrise view from Ahihi-Kinau.

2 Longhi's. I love to sit in the open air and sip a latte and munch on Longhi's fresh baked cinnamon rolls (one is enough for two people). Big eaters may want to try the eggs Benedict or Florentine with a light but flavorful hollandaise and perfect baguettes. *The Shops at Wailea, 3750 Wailea Alanui Dr., Wailea.* ☎ *808/891-8883. www.longhi-maui. com. Breakfast $8.50–$20; lunch $8.50–$30; dinner $28–$80. AE, DC, MC, V. Breakfast, lunch & dinner daily.*

Retrace your route back to Makena Rd. and head toward Makena Landing Beach Park, a distance of 2 miles (3.2km).

1 ★ Ahihi-Kinau. La Pérouse Monument is a pyramid of lava rocks that marks the spot where the first Westerner to "discover" the island, French explorer Admiral Comte de La Pérouse, set foot on Maui in 1786. Park here, and if you're up for it, start your hike. Bring plenty of water and sun protection, and wear hiking boots that can withstand walking on lava. From La Pérouse Bay, you can pick up the old **King's Highway trail,** which once circled the island. Walk along the sandy beach at La Pérouse; if the water is calm, take a swim, but if it's rough, just enjoy the view. Look for the trail indentation in the lava at the end of the sandy beach, which leads down to the lighthouse at the tip of Cape Hanamanioa, about a ¾ of a mile (1.2km) round-trip. Give yourself an hour or two to spend in the peace and quiet of this wilderness area.

Retrace your route back to Makena Rd. Go left on Makena Alanui Rd., which becomes Wailea Alnui Rd. at The Shops at Wailea, about 3 miles (4.8km).

3 ★ Makena. This beach park with boat-launching facilities, showers, toilets, and picnic tables, has generally calm waters teeming with colorful tropical fish. It's the perfect place for beginner kayakers and snorkelers. Dino Ventura of **Makena Kayak Tours** (p 106), specializes in teaching first-time kayakers. For one of the more history-rich stops in this area, go south on Makena Road from the landing; on the right is ★ **Keawali Congregational Church** (☎ 808/879-5557), built in 1855. Surrounded by ti leaves, which by Hawaiian custom provide protection, and built of 3-foot (0.9m) thick lava rock with coral for mortar, this Protestant church sits on its own cove with a golden-sand beach. It's not always open, but you can view the inside on Sunday during the 9:30am Hawaiian-language service. Take some time to wander through the cemetery, where you'll see some tombstones with ceramic pictures of the deceased, an old custom.

Retrace your route back to Makena Rd. Go left on Makena Alanui Rd., which becomes Wailea Alnui

Rd. Look for the blue sign noting Public Beach Access. It's in about 2 miles (3.2km).

④ ★ Wailea. Leaving the past in Makena, we're on to the present with the multi-million dollar high-rise luxury resorts that line the 2 miles (3.2km) of this palm-fringed gold coast. For an up-close look, park in the public beach access lot and walk the oceanfront, 3-mile (4.8km) round-trip path, which has terrific views of both the ocean and the lushly landscaped resorts. Allow about an hour for this stroll along Maui's most expensive properties.

Go left on Wailea Alanui Rd. and left again at stop sign to Okolani Dr., which becomes Kihei Rd. It's about 3½ miles (5.6km).

⑤ kids Joy's Place. Stop for lunch at this tiny eatery with healthy, delicious lunches (huge sandwiches, wraps, fresh salads, soups, and desserts) at rock-bottom prices. My picks are the falafel burger or the spinach quinoa burger. The deli has a few seats, but the beach is just across the street. *Island Surf Building, 1993 S. Kihei Rd., Kihei (entrance to the restaurant is on Auhana St.).* ☎ *808/879-9258. All items under $10. No credit cards. Mon–Sat 10am–5pm.*

Continue north on Kihei Rd. for 2½ miles (4km).

⑥ Kihei. Kihei is a nearly continuous series of condos and minimalls lining Kihei Road. However, a couple of terrific places showcase island wildlife. To get some background on the whales that visit Hawaii from December to April, stop by the **Hawaii Humpback Whale Sanctuary Center,** 725 Kihei Rd (☎ 808/879-2818; www.hawaiihumpback-whale.noaa.gov). This small educational center has dozens of exhibits, artifacts, and displays on whales, turtles, and other ocean life. Allow about 30 minutes here, then continue on Kihei Rd. north to **Kealia Pond National Wildlife Preserve** (☎ 808/875-1582), a 700-acre (280-hectare) U.S. Fish and Wildlife wetland preserve. This is a fantastic place to see many endangered Hawaiian species like the black-crowned high heron, and Hawaiian stilts, coots, and ducks. The best time to visit is from July to December, when hawksbill turtles come ashore to lay their eggs. You can take a self-guided tour along a boardwalk dotted with interpretive signs and shade shelters, through sand dunes, and around ponds to Maalaea Harbor. The boardwalk starts at the outlet of Kealia Pond on the ocean side of North Kihei Rd.

Wildlife at Kealia Pond.

Maui Ocean Center.

(near MM 2 on Hwy. 31). Allow at least an hour, longer if the turtles are around.

Continue north on Hwy. 31, then go left on Hwy. 30 to the Maalaea turn off. It's about 3 miles (4.8km).

⑦ ★★★ kids Maui Ocean Center. The windy oceanfront village of Maalaea centers on a small boat harbor (with a general store, a couple of restaurants, and a huge new mall) and the Maui Ocean Center, an aquarium/ocean complex. This 5-acre facility houses the largest aquarium in Hawaii. My favorite section is the aquarium's centerpiece: a 100-foot- (30m) long, 750,000-gallon tank featuring tiger, gray, and white-tip sharks, as well as tuna, surgeonfish, triggerfish, and numerous tropical fish. The aquarium is set up so you feel as though you are descending from the "beach" to the deepest part of the ocean. A walkway goes right through the tank, so you're surrounded on three sides by marine creatures. If you're a certified scuba diver, you can participate in the **Shark Dive Maui Program,** which allows you (for a fee of $190) to plunge into the aquarium and swim with the sharks, stingrays, and tropical fish. 🕐 *2 hours or more. Maalaea Harbor Village, 192 Maalaea Rd. (the triangle between Honoapiilani Hwy. and Maalaea Rd.)* ☎ *808/270-7000; www.mauiocean center.com. Buy your tickets online to avoid the long admission lines. Admission $22 adults, $19 seniors, $15 children 3–12. Daily 9am–5pm (until 6pm July–Aug).*

⑧ kids The Waterfront at Maalaea. Stop for dinner at this family-owned restaurant, known for its fresh seafood, which is caught in nearby Maalaea Harbor. I recommend any of the fresh fish (with nine different preparations). Vegetarian and meat entrees are also available. Dessert is baked fresh daily; my favorite is the double chocolate brownie with vanilla ice cream. Try to come around sunset, when the harbor views are stunning. *Maalaea Harbor, 50 Hauoli St.* ☎ *808/244-9028. www.waterfrontrestaurant. net. Reservations recommended. Main courses $19–$38. AE, DC, DISC, MC, V. Dinner daily.*

Central Maui

This flat, often windy corridor between Maui's two volcanoes is the site of the main airport, where you'll probably arrive. It's also home to the majority of the island's population, the heart of the business community, and center of the local government (courts, cops, and county/state government agencies). You'll find good shopping and dining bargains as well. START: Wailuku. Trip length: 2½ miles (4km)

❶ ★ Wailuku. With its faded wooden storefronts, old plantation homes, and shops straight out of the 1940s, quaint little Wailuku is worth a brief visit for its history and architecture. Take a couple of hours to wander around. See p 44.

Take Main St. west to Valley Rd., about 3.5 miles (5.6km).

❷ ★★ kids Iao Valley. A 2,250-foot (686-m) needle pricks the clouds scudding across the sky. The air is moist and cool, and the shade

a welcome comfort. This is Iao Valley, (Iao means "Supreme Light") the eroded volcanic caldera of the West Maui Mountains and a 6-acre (2.4-hectare) state park. The head of the Iao Valley is a broad circular amphitheater where four major streams converge into **Iao Stream** (a great place for kids to splash around). At the back of the amphitheater is rain-drenched **Puu Kukui,** the West Maui Mountains' highest point. No other Hawaiian valley lets you go from seacoast to

Iao Valley.

rainforest so easily. This peaceful valley, full of tropical plants, rainbows, waterfalls, swimming holes, and hiking trails (two of them paved and easy), is a place of solitude, reflection, and escape. Pack a picnic, take your swim suit, spend a couple of hours. *Iao Valley State Park, 54 S. High St., Wailuku (☎ 808/ 984-8109).Open daily 10am-4pm.*

Retrace your route to the light at Main St. and Hwy. 30, turn left and drive 3 miles (4.8km) south on Hwy. 30.

❸ kids **Waikapu.** The tiny, single-street village of Waikapu has at least one attraction that's worth checking out: the 40-minute narrated tram ride around fields of pineapple, sugar cane, and papaya trees at **Maui Tropical Plantation** (p 39) that allows you to relive Maui's past. Make sure that you have at least an hour to spend here; you'll want to check out their country store before you leave.

Head north on Hwy. 30, go right on Waiko Rd, and go left on Hwy. 380 to Kahului. Parking for the Kanana Wildlife Sanctuary is behind the mall, across from Cutter Automotive, where hwys. 37/36 intersect. It's about 4 miles (6.4km).

❹ **Kahului.** As you drive through Maui's most populated town, look out on the miles of subdivisions: this is "Dream City," home to thousands of former sugar-cane workers who dreamed of owning their own homes away from the plantations. Despite a few shopping opportunities (p 135), this is not a place to spend your vacation. However, one attraction that is worth visiting—incongruously located under the airport flight path, next to Maui's busiest intersection and across from Costco in Kahului's new business park—is the **Kanaha Wildlife Sanctuary** (Haleakala Hwy. Ext. & Hana Hwy; ☎ 808/984-8100). A 150-foot trail meanders along the shore to a shade shelter and lookout to the permanent home of the endangered black-neck Hawaiian stilt, whose population is now down to about 1,000 to 1,500. Naturalists say this is a good place to see endangered Hawaiian Koloa ducks, stilts, coots, and other migrating shorebirds. Plan a quick 10-minute drive through the town and another 15 minutes wandering the Wildlife Sanctuary.

Take Hwy. 36 to the intersection, go right on Daily Rd., left on Puunene Ave., and left on Hansen Rd. It's about 2 miles (3.2km).

❺ **Puunene.** To soak up a little more of Maui's colorful history, drive out to this town in the middle of the central Maui plains. Once a thriving sugar-plantation town with hundreds of homes, a school, a shopping area, and a community center, Puunene today consists of little more than a sugar mill, a post office, and a museum (the **Alexander & Baldwin Sugar Museum**, p 45). You can tour the museum in 15 minutes, then step outside, breathe in the smells of the nearby sugar mill, and watch the green sugar cane blowing in the wind. This is a part of Maui that is quickly disappearing.

Wailuku

1 Wailuku Elementary School
2 Wailuku Union Church
3 Wailuku Public Library
4 Territorial Building
5 Kaahumanu Church
6 Bailey House Museum
7 Cemetery
8 Iao Congregational Church
9 Vineyard Street
10 Maui Bake Shop
11 Market Street
12 Iao Theater
13 Hoapili Hale
14 Old State Court House
15 Maui County Building
16 Old County Building

The town of Wailuku, which most visitors merely glance at through their car windows as they whiz past on the way to Iao Valley, has played a significant role in Maui's history over the past 225 years. One of Hawaii's bloodiest battles took place here in 1790, when Kamehameha the Great fought the Maui chiefs in his bid to unite the Hawaiian Islands. The carnage was so intense that 4-mile-(6.4km-) long Iao Stream turned red from the slaughter, hence the name Wailuku ("bloody waters"). Wailuku was also where the missionaries landed in the mid-1800s to "save" the natives and convert them to Christianity. This quaint community still retains the New England architectural influences the settlers brought with them. **START: A town tour starts and ends at the Wailuku Elementary School on High Street. Trip Length: 2 miles (3.2km). Allow a couple of hours**

1 **Wailuku Elementary School.** This old stone building housing Maui school children since 1904 was designed by C. W. Dickey, once one of Hawaii's most prolific architects. His distinctive double-hipped roof style can be seen in several buildings in this old town. After school or on weekends you can walk around the outside of the old building. *355 S. High St.* ☎ *808/984-5622.*

2 **Wailuku Union Church.** This brick structure was built in 1911 and

still holds church services every Sunday at 10am. Visitors are welcome to come inside. *327 S. High St.* ☎ *808/244-9177.*

3 **Wailuku Public Library.** Step inside to see the architectural details of this early 20th-century building also designed by C. W. Dickey. By 1928, when he designed this building, Dickey had modified his California Mission style to meet Hawaii's climate and cultural needs, incorporating large openings and comparatively small wall spaces to allow tradewinds to enter. Dickey also was a fan of big porches and wide, hanging eaves to protect the inside from frequent showers, and eliminate the need to close the windows. *251 S. High St.* ☎ *808/243-5766.*

4 **Territorial Building.** Still another C. W. Dickey design, built in 1930, and once home to the Territory of Hawaii government. This is a great example of Dickey's work, with the trademark wide, overhanging eaves. Dickey never claimed to have originated this form, called a double-pitched hip roof, but over the years he used it in so many of his designs that it is now called the "Dickey" or "Hawaiian" roof. Although different from the steep roof of the old Hawaiian grass house, the two have similar visual impact—both use plain broad surfaces to emphasize volume. The building is open during weekday working hours; step inside and see his handiwork close up. *151 S. High St.*

Maui's Early History

The first Hawaiian settlers arrived by canoe, part of the great Polynesian migration. No one is sure when they arrived, but artifacts at the Maluuluolele Park in Lahaina date back to between A.D. 700 and 900.

All we have today are archaeological finds, some scientific data, and ancient chants to tell the story of Hawaii's past. The chants, especially the *Kumulipo*, which is the chant of creation and the litany of genealogy of the *alii* (high-ranking chiefs) who ruled the islands, talk about journeys between Hawaii and the islands of the south, presumed to be Tahiti.

Around 1300, the transoceanic voyages stopped and Hawaii began to develop its own culture. The settlers built temples, fishponds, and aqueducts to irrigate taro plantations. Each island was a separate kingdom. The *alii* created a caste system and established taboos. High priests asked the gods Lono and Ku for divine guidance. Ritual human sacrifices were common.

Maui's history is one of wars and conquests, with one chief capturing another's land. The rugged terrain of Maui and the water separating Maui, Molokai, Lanai, and Kahoolawe made good natural boundaries. In the early years there were three kingdoms on Maui: Hana, Waikulu, and Lahaina.

In the early 15th century, a ruler from Hana became the first to unite Maui. Piilani's rule was a time of peace; he built fishponds and irrigation fields and began creating a paved road around the island.

Kaahumanu Church.

5 ★ Kaahumanu Church.

Named after Queen Kaahumanu, the monarch whose conversion to Christianity prompted thousands of her subjects to follow her lead, this was one of Maui's first stone churches. Originally it was a grass-hut, but in 1837 the hut was replaced by a stone structure designed by architect-artist Edward Bailey (see 6). The current church was built in 1876. If it's open, step inside to see the austere New England–style interior. Be sure to visit the small cemetery, containing the graves of the first missionaries. *103 High St.* ☎ *808/244-5189.*

6 ★★ Bailey House Museum.

This 1840s building housed Hawaii's first boarding school for girls, the Wailuku Female Seminary, with Edward Bailey as the principal. Bailey went on to manage the Wailuku Sugar Company, but he is also known as a prolific landscape painter, depicting Maui from 1866 to 1886. I love this old Hawaiian home and could spend hours combing through the collection of Hawaiian artifacts, furniture, clothing, and tools from the missionary era. Don't miss the gift store's fabulous finds and great

buys. ⏱ *30–45 min. 2375-A Main St.* ☎ *808/244-3326; www.mauimuseum. org. Admission $5 adults, $4 seniors, $1 children 7–12, free for children 6 and under. Mon–Sat 10am–4pm.*

7 Cemetery.

The names engraved on the tombstones here are like a record of Wailuku's immigration history in miniature, a snapshot of the various ethnic groups that flocked to Maui during the sugar boom years. Before you leave, stop and admire the view of Iao Valley and the West Maui Mountains. ⏱ *10–15 mins. Ilima at Vineyard sts.*

8 Iao Congregational Church.

Missionaries played a major role in Maui's history and this 1895 church continues to be very active in the community. *2371 Vineyard St.* ☎ *808/244-7353.*

9 Vineyard Street.

This eclectic street, especially between Ilina and Market sts., consists of old plantation houses, a few defunct stores, thriving small businesses, and beautifully restored buildings, next door to dilapidated shacks.

10 kids Maui Bake Shop.

The owners turn out buttery brioches, healthy nine-grain and two-tone rye breads, focaccia, strudels, sumptuous fresh-fruit gâteaux, and puff pastries. I always go for a cup of coffee and a slice of the wonderful white-chocolate macadamia-nut cheesecake. *2092 Vineyard St., Wailuku.* ☎ *808/242-0064. Most items under $5. AE, DISC, MC, V. Breakfast & lunch Mon–Sat.*

11 Market Street.

Local residents call this street Antique Row, for the curious, collectibles, memorabilia, and antique shops that line it.

12 ★ Iao Theater.

Opened in 1928 and built in Spanish Mission

Where the Locals Eat

In the northern section of Wailuku, **Takamiya Market,** 359 N. Market St. (☎ 808/244-3404), is much loved by local folks as the place to stock up on picnic fare and mouthwatering ethnic foods. From the chilled-fish counter come fresh sashimi and *poke* (raw fish with seaweed and onions), and an assortment of prepared foods like shoyu chicken, tender fried squid, roast pork, Kalua pork, laulau, Chinese noodles, fiddlehead ferns, and Western comfort foods, such as corn bread and potato salad.

style, this theater was once Wailuku's main entertainment venue. Although threatened with demolition in the early 1980s, the theater eventually underwent a million dollar–plus renovation and was placed on the National Register of Historic Places in 1995. It's now home to **Maui OnStage,** which produces and hosts live theater and other events. It's generally closed during the day, but you can come back in the evening and see a production. *68 N. Market St.* ☎ *808/244-8680; www.mauionstage.com.*

⓮ Hoapili Hale. This, one of the few modern buildings in the old town, houses the state courts. It's open weekdays, and you are welcome to go inside and see which you prefer, the old Wailuku or the new Wailuku. *2145 Main St.* ☎ *808/244-2800.*

⓮ Old State Court House. Built in 1907, this regal old court house was hearing trials up until a

few years ago, when all court activity moved to Hoapili Hale. While it's open weekdays to house various state agencies, regretfully little of the interior of the turn-of-the-20th-century rooms remains. *190 S. High St.*

⓯ Maui County Building. This nine-story concrete structure stands out (some say like a sore thumb) among the historic buildings surrounding it. When it was built in the early 1970s the mayor at the time said he wanted it to be the biggest building in Wailuku—well, he got his wish. *200 S. High St.*

⓰ Old County Building. This stone edifice, built in 1929, was once large enough to serve all the needs of Maui County. While it's not exactly in the Dickey style, it's close enough to give you an idea of what Wailuku looked like in the early 20th century, shortly after the monarchy was overthrown. It is open weekdays during working hours, and you are welcome to wander inside. *210 S. High St.*

Bailey House Museum.

Upcountry Maui

A fter a few days at the beach, you'll probably be ready to explore the 10,000-foot (3,000km) mountain in the middle of Maui. The slopes of Haleakala are home to cowboys, farmers, and other welcoming country people. Crisp air, emerald pastures, eucalyptus, flower farms, even a misty California redwood grove are the highlights of this tropical Olympus. START: **Makawao. Trip Length: 24 miles (38.6km), but plan on a full day**

1 ★ Makawao. Until recently, this small, two-street town consisted of little more than a post office, a gas station, a feed store, a bakery, a restaurant/bar, and hitching posts for horses. As the population of Maui started expanding in the 1970s, however, a health-food store popped up, followed by boutiques and a host of health-conscious restaurants. The result is an eclectic amalgam of old *paniolo* (cowboy) Hawaii and the baby-boomer trends of transplanted

mainlanders. Spend the morning looking at the unusual shops. Don't miss my favorite, **Hui No'eau Visual Arts Center** (p 138), Hawaii's premier arts collective.

Take Makawao Ave. to the light at Hwy. 37, turn left, and head up the mountain. Go left on Hwy. 377. It will take about 25 minutes.

2 Kula Lodge. Take a lunch break here not only for the food, but for

Hui No'eau Visual Arts Center.

the million-dollar vista that spans the flanks of Haleakala, central Maui, the ocean, and the West Maui Mountains. My favorites are the Kula onion soup (with Maui's famous sweet onions) and the clubhouse sandwich (smoked turkey on a homemade bun with homemade spicy orange B.B.Q. sauce). *Haleakala Hwy. (Hwy. 377).* ☎ *808/878-2517.* $$.

Retrace your route on Hwy. 377, then go left on Hwy. 37. It's a 5-minute drive to Alii Kula Lavender, and about 20–30 minutes from there to Surfing Goat Dairy.

❸ ★ **Kula.** Continue south through the bucolic rolling hills of this pastoral upcountry community of old flower farms, humble cottages, and new suburban ranch houses with million-dollar views that take in the ocean, isthmus, West Maui Mountains, Lanai, and Kahoolawe off in the distance. Kula sits at a cool 3,000 feet (914m), just below the cloud line, and from here a winding road snakes its way up to Haleakala National Park. Everyone in this area grows something—Maui onions, carnations, orchids, and proteas, those strange-looking blossoms that look like *Star Trek* props.

Must-stops are: **Alii Kula Lavender** (p 32) and kids **Surfing Goat Dairy** (p 26).

Continue on Hwy. 37 for 14 miles (22.5km).

❹ ★ **Ulupalakua.** The final stop on the upcountry tour is on the southern shoulder of Haleakala, **Ulupalakua Ranch,** a 20,000-acre (8,000 hectare) spread once owned by legendary sea captain James Makee. The ranch is now home to Maui's only **winery,** established in 1974 by Napa vintner Emil Tedeschi. Stop in the tasting room and sample Maui's wines (pass on the pineapple wines—Maui Splash and Maui Blanc—yuck!). Across from the winery are the remains of the three smokestacks of the **Makee Sugar Mill,** built in 1878. This is home to Maui artist Reems Mitchell, who carved the mannequins on the front porch of the Ulupalakua Ranch Store: a Filipino with his fighting cock, a cowboy, a farmhand, and a sea captain, all representing the people of Maui's history. (When you drive past you'll swear they're real.) *Tedeschi Vineyards and Winery, off Hwy. 37 (Kula Hwy.).* ☎ *808/878-6058; www.mauiwine.com. Daily 9am–5pm. Free tastings; tours given 10:30am–1:30pm.*

The **Road to Hana**

1 Kahului
2 Charley's
3 Hookipa Beach Park
4 Jaws
5 Maui Grown Market and Deli
6 Twin Falls
7 Huelo
8 Waikamoi Ridge
9 Kaumahina State Wayside Park
10 Keanae Arboretum
11 Keanae Peninsula
12 Kaenae Lookout
13 Uncle Harry's Fruit & Flower Stand
14 Wailua
15 Wailua Valley State Wayside Park
16 Puaa Kaa State Wayside Park
17 Nahiku
18 Nahiku Coffee Shop

Top down, sunscreen on, swimming suit handy, radio tuned to a Hawaiian music station on a Maui morning: It's time to head out to Hana along the Hana Highway (Hwy. 36). This wiggle of a road winds for 50 miles (80.5km) along Maui's northeastern shore, passing taro patches, magnificent seascapes, waterfall pools, botanical gardens, and verdant rainforests. Bring a few beach towels, a picnic lunch, and your camera. START: Kahului. Trip length: 50 miles (80.5km). The drive takes at least 3 hours, but to really enjoy the trip, plan to spend all day

1 Fueling up in Kahului. This is the cheapest place to get gas. Don't wait until Paia, the last place for gas before the long trip to Hana, because it's incredibly expensive.

Continue on the Hana Hwy. for 8 miles (12.9km).

2 kids Charley's. Pull into quaint Paia for a big, hearty breakfast at a reasonable price. *142 Hana Hwy., Paia.* ☎ *808/579-9453. $-$$.*

Continue on the Hana Hwy. until just before MM 9.

3 ★ kids Hookipa Beach Park. See p 76.

Detour off the Hana Hwy. left at Hahana Rd., between MM 13 and 14. Don't park on the pineapples!

4 ★★ kids Jaws. If it's winter and conditions are right, expert tow-in surfers battle the mammoth waves off Pauwela at an area known as Jaws (because the waves will chew you up).

The Road to Hana.

Just before MM 15.

5 Maui Grown Market and Deli. This is my pick for the best "bang for your buck" picnic lunch: a mere $8.95 gets you a sandwich (my favorite is the avo-veggie, but they also have pastrami, roast beef, turkey, and tuna), with two cookies, a mac nut candy bar, chips or fruit, and soda or water. *Hana Hwy.* ☎ *808/572-1693. $.*

After MM 16, the road is still called the Hana Highway, but the number changes from Hwy. 36 to Hwy. 360, and the MMs go back to 0. Stop at MM 2.

6 Twin Falls. Pull over on the mountain side and park; the waterfall and pool are a 3- to 5- minute walk. The mountain stream water is a bit chilly when you first get in, but it's good for swimming. If it's crowded, keep going, plenty of other swimming holes and waterfalls are coming up.

Just before MM 4, on a blind curve, look for a double row of mailboxes on the left.

7 Huelo. This is a great side trip to see some of Maui's history. Down the road lies a hidden Hawaii, where an indescribable sense of serenity prevails. Hemmed in by Waipo and Hoalua bays is the remote community of Huelo. This fertile area once supported a population of 75,000; today only a few hundred live here. Stop in at the historic 1853 **Kaulanapueo Church.**

Continue to MM 9.

8 kids Waikamoi Ridge. This small state wayside area with restrooms, picnic tables, and a barbecue area has an easy ¾-mile (1.2km) loop-trail hike. It starts just behind the "quiet trees at work" sign.

Just past MM 12:

9 kids Kaumahina State Wayside Park. This is not only a good pit stop (restrooms are available) and a wonderful place for the picnic you picked up earlier, but it also offers wonderful views and a great photo op of the rugged coastline all the way down to the jutting Keanae Peninsula.

Between MMs 16 and 17.

10 ★★ kids Keanae Arboretum. Here the region's botany is divided into three parts: native forest; introduced forest; and traditional Hawaiian plants, food, and medicine. You can swim in the pools of Piinaau Stream or walk a mile-long trail into Keanae Valley's tropical rainforest.

11 ★★★ kids Keanae Peninsula. The old Hawaiian village of **Keanae** stands out against the Pacific like a place time forgot. This is one of the last coastal enclaves of native Hawaiians. Be sure to visit the **Kaenae Congregational Church** (☎ 808/248-8040). Built in 1860 of lava rocks and coral mortar, it stands in stark contrast to the surrounding green fields.

Just past MM 17.

12 kids Kaenae Lookout. Get the camera out: Here you can see the entire Keanae Peninsula's checkerboard pattern of green taro fields and its ocean boundary etched in black lava.

Around MM 18:

13 Uncle Harry's Fruit & Flower Stand. Around MM 18 you'll start to see numerous small stands selling fruit or flowers. Many stands work on the honor system. My favorite, Uncle Harry's, sells a variety of fruits and juices Monday through Saturday.

Just after Uncle Harry's, look for the Wailua Road off on the left.

14 Wailua. Behind pink St. Gabriel's Church is the smaller, blue-and-white **Coral Miracle Church,** home of the **Our Lady of Fatima Shrine.** According to legend, in 1860 the men of this village were diving to collect coral to build a

Make sure to pull off at a waterfall or two for an impromptu swim.

An overview of the Kaenae Peninsula.

church. But the coral offshore was in deep water and the men could only retrieve a few pieces at a time, making construction an arduous project. Then a freak storm hit the area and deposited the deep-sea coral on a nearby beach, allowing the Hawaiians to easily complete the church.

Just before MM 19:

15 ★ kids Wailua Valley State Wayside Park. Climb the stairs for a view of the Keanae Valley, waterfalls, and Wailua Peninsula. On a really clear day, you can see up the mountain to the Koolau Gap.

Between MMs 22 and 23.

16 kids Puaa Kaa State Wayside Park. The sound of waterfalls provides the background music for this small park area with restrooms, a phone, and a picnic area. There's a well-marked path to the falls and to a swimming hole. Ginger plants are everywhere: Pick some flowers and put them in your car so that you can travel with their sweet smell.

Just after MM 25 is a narrow 3-mile (4.8km) road leading from the highway, at about 1,000 feet (300m) elevation, down to sea level.

17 Nahiku. This remote, stunningly beautiful area was once a thriving village of thousands; today the population has dwindled to fewer than a hundred—including a few Hawaiian families, but mostly extremely wealthy mainland residents who jet in for a few weeks at a time. At the end of the road, you can see the remains of the old wharf from the town's rubber-plantation days. There's a small picnic area off to the side. Dolphins are frequently seen in the bay.

Go ½ mile (0.8km) past MM 28 on the ocean side of the road.

18 Nahiku Coffee Shop. What a delight to stumble across this small coffee shop with locally made baked goods, Maui-grown coffee, banana bread, organic tropical-fruit smoothies, and my favorite, the Original and Best Coconut Candy. While you are here, check out the **Smoked Fish Stand**, a great place to stock up on superb smoked and grilled fish. Next door the **Ti Gallery** sells locally made Hawaiian arts and crafts. *Hana Hwy., ½ mile past MM 28.* **No phone. $.**

A fruit stand on the way to Hana.

Hana

1 Waianapanapa State Park
2 Kahanu Garden
3 Hana Cultural Center and Museum
4 Hasegawa General Store
5 Hana Bay
6 Hotel Hana-Maui
7 Fagan's Cross
8 Wananalua Congregation Church
9 Hana Ranch Center
10 Oheo Gulch
11 Lindbergh's Grave
12 Kaupo

Green, tropical Hana is a destination all its own, a small coastal village that's probably what you came to Maui in search of. Here you'll find a rainforest punctuated with cascading waterfalls and sparkling blue pools, skirted by red- and black-sand beaches. Hana enjoys more than 90 inches of rain a year—more than enough to keep the scenery lush. Banyans, bamboo, breadfruit trees—everything seems larger than life in this small town, especially the wild ginger and plumeria flowers. Most visitors will zip through Hana, perhaps taking a quick look out their car windows at a few sights before buzzing on down the road. They might think they've seen Hana, but they definitely haven't experienced its true beauty and serenity. **START: Hana. Trip length: only 12 miles (19.3km), but at least 2 or 3 days**

Travel Tip

Try to see Hana's attractions, especially the pools, ponds, and waterfalls, early in the day. You'll have them all to yourself. The day-tourists arrive in Hana around 11am and stay until about 4pm; during that window, the area is overrun with hundreds and hundreds of people, all in a hurry, and all wanting to pack Hana's sights into just a few hours.

From Hwy. 360 turn toward the ocean on Ulaino Rd., by MM 32. The drive takes about 5 minutes.

❶ ★★★ kids Waianapanapa State Park. Get up early to see shiny black-sand Waianapanapa Beach and hike the coastal trail. Plan to spend at least a couple of hours at this 120-acre (49-hectare) park that appears like a vivid dream, with bright-green jungle foliage on three sides and cobalt-blue water lapping at its shore. Swimming is not the best here (rough seas, strong currents), but you can hike a trail (p 82) along the ancient lava flow that passes by sea cliffs, lava tubes, arches, and the beach. *End of Waianapanapa Rd. off Hana Hwy. (Hwy. 360), Hana (☎ 808/248-4843). Open daily 24 hours.*

The black sand at Waianapanapa Beach.

Follow Hwy. 360, then turn right to MM 31 for ⅕ mile (0.3km).

❷ ★★ kids Kahanu Garden. Plan to arrive when the gates open at 10am to have plenty of time to explore this 472-acre (191-hectare) garden, including the largest known collection of breadfruit trees in the world. The real draw here is the huge **Piilanihale Heiau** (House of Piilani), temple to one of Maui's greatest chiefs. Believed to be the largest temple in the state, this structure's mammoth proportions—340-feet by 415-feet (102m by 124.5m), with walls 50-feet (15m) tall and 8- to 10-feet (2.4m–3m) thick—are humbling.

Torch Ginger at Kahanu Garden.

Historians believe that Piilani's two sons and his grandson built the enormous temple, which was dedicated to war, sometime in the 1500s. ⏱ *1 hour. Ulaino Rd.* ☎ *808/248-8912; www.ntbg.org. Open Monday–Friday from 10am–2pm, admission is $10 for self-guided tours.*

· As you enter Hana, the road splits about ½ mile (0.8km) past MM 33, at the police station. Both roads will take you to Hana, but Uakea Rd. is more scenic.

❸ ★ kids Hana Cultural Center and Museum. With the sun starting to reach its zenith, take a cooling break while touring this small museum's excellent collection of Hawaiian quilts, artifacts, books, and photos. Kids will love the **Kauhala O Hana,** consisting of four *hale* (houses) for living, meeting, cooking, and canoe building or canoe storage. ⏱ *30 min. 4974 Uakea Rd.* ☎ *808/248-8622; http://hookele.com/hccm. Daily from 10am–4pm.*

Turn toward the mountains at Keawa Place, then go left on Hwy. 360 for a ½ mile (0.8km).

❹ Hasegawa General Store. Time for lunch. Hana doesn't have a lot of culinary opportunities (and the few that exist are either very expensive, or not that appetizing). I usually head for this legendary general store, established in 1910, immortalized in song since 1961, to find some picnic items (chips, fruit, cookies, soda, bread, lunch fixings). The aisles are choked with merchandise: organic dried fruit, every type of soda and juice you can imagine, a variety of breads and lunch meats, baby food, napkins, and other necessities. You could spend a good 20 minutes just marveling at all of the products they cram into this tiny space. Then head to Hana Bay for a picnic. *Hwy. 360, Hana.* ☎ *808/248-8231.*

Trace your route back to Ukea Rd., turn right to the bay. It's less than ½ mile (0.8km).

❺ ★ kids Hana Bay. You'll find restrooms, showers, picnic tables, barbecue areas, and even a snack bar (which I would pass up—it's expensive and not the best cuisine on Maui). Enjoy watching the activities in the bay—fishermen, surfers, swimmers, and beach combers—as you eat your lunch. Then take a short, 5- to 10-minute after-lunch hike. Look for the 386-foot (115.8km), red-faced cinder cone beside the bay. This is **Kauiki Hill,** site of numerous fierce battles in ancient Hawaii and the birthplace of Queen Kaahumanu in 1768, who played a huge roll in Hawaii's history by encouraging her people to convert from the old religion to Christianity. A leisurely stroll will take you to her birthplace. Look for the trail along the hill on the wharf side, and follow the path through the ironwood trees; the lighthouse on the point will come into view, and you'll see pocket beaches of red cinder below. Honeymooners might want to picnic in this romantic secluded spot.

Cross Uakea Rd., and drive up Keawa Place; turn left on Hwy. 360. It's less than ½ mile (0.8km).

6 Hotel Hana-Maui. If you can afford it, this is THE place to stay in Hana (and one of the state's top resorts). If they aren't too busy, the staff generally is amenable to taking you on a tour in their speedy golf carts. They have an elegant spa here, too. Plan on half hour to see this elegant resort, longer if you want to get a meal or a drink at one of the restaurants here. See p 115.

On the green hills above Hotel Hana-Maui:

7 kids Fagan's Cross. If you have a carload of kids and don't think they'd settle down long enough to tour the Hotel Hana-Maui, then take them for a hike up this hill to the 30-foot- (9m-) high white cross (made of lava rock), erected in memory of Paul Fagan, who founded the Hana Ranch as well as the Hotel Hana-Maui. The 3-mile- (4.8km-) round-trip hike provides a gorgeous view of the Hana coast, especially at sunset. The uphill trail starts across Hana Hwy. from the Hotel Hana-Maui. (Enter the pastures at your own risk; they're often occupied by glaring bulls and cows with new calves.) Watch your step as you ascend this steep hill. The hike can take 1 to 2 hours, depending on how fast you hike and how long you linger at the top admiring the breathtaking view.

Back on Hwy. 30, just past Hauoli Rd. about ¼ mile (0.4km).

8 Wananalua Congregation Church. Stop in and see this historic church, built from coral stones from 1838 to 1842 during the missionary rush to convert the natives. But be aware: Hawaiians whisper among themselves that it was built atop an old Hawaiian *heiau* (temple),

considered not very politically correct today. 🕐 *15 minutes. Hwy. 30, just past Hauoli Rd.*

Just past the church, on the right side of Hwy. 30.

9 Hana Ranch Center. This small cluster of one-story buildings is Hana's commercial center, with a post office, bank, general store, the Hana Ranch Stables, and a restaurant and snack bar. If you are hungry or thirsty they can help you out here. *Hwy. 30.*

Continue past Hana on Hwy. 31 for 8 miles (12.9km).

10 ★★★ kids Oheo Gulch. Time to hit the water again. This is the Kipahulu end of Haleakala National Park. For years people called this series of stair-step waterfalls and pools "Seven Sacred Pools." There are more than 7 pools—about 24, actually—and *all* water in Hawaii is considered sacred. Don't miss my favorite spot, magnificent 400-foot (120m) **Waimoku Falls,** reachable via an often-muddy, but rewarding, hour-long uphill hike. The Kipahulu rangers offer safety information, exhibits, books, and a variety of walks and hikes year-round; check at the station for current activities. Expect showers on the Kipahulu coast. ☎ *808/248-7375; www.nps.gov/hale. Fee is $5 per person or $10 per car.*

Wananalua Church with Fagan's Cross in the background.

Waimoku Falls.

Continue a mile past Oheo Gulch on the ocean side of Hwy. 31.

⓫ Lindbergh's Grave. Visitors of a certain generation—as well as those interested in the history of aviation—make the trek to honor renowned aviator Charles A. Lindbergh (1902–74), who was the first to fly across the Atlantic. He settled in Kipahulu, where he died of cancer in 1974, and was buried under river stones in a seaside graveyard

Oheo Gulch.

behind the 1857 **Palapala Hoomau Congregational Church.** You'll have no trouble finding his tombstone, which is engraved with his favorite words from the 139th Psalm: "If I take the wings of the morning and dwell in the uttermost parts of the sea . . ."

About 5 miles (8km) farther down on Hwy. 31.

⓬ Kaupo. If you still have daylight you can continue on (or you can wait until the next day) to the highlights of remote, rural Kaupo. These include the restored 1859 **Huialoha Congregationalist "Circuit" Church,** where the view of the ocean is the main attraction; and farther down the road, the **Kaupo Store,** an eclectic old country store that carries a range of bizarre goods and doesn't keep any of its posted hours, but is a fun place to "talk story" with the staff about this area, which at one time had quite a population. ☎ *808/248-8054. Store hours are officially Monday–Friday from 7:30am–4:30pm, but in this arid cattle country, posted store hours often prove meaningless.* ●

Beaches Best Bets

Best **Black Sand**
★ Waianapanapa State Park, MM 32
Hana Hwy. (Hwy. 360), Hana (p 82).

Best for **Body Surfing**
★ H. A. Baldwin Park, MM 6 Hana
Hwy. (Hwy. 360), between Spreckels-
ville and Paia (p 79), and ★★ Hamoa
Beach, Haneoo Rd., Hana (p 78).

Best for **Solitude**
★★ D. T. Fleming Beach Park,
Honoapiilani Hwy. (Hwy. 30),
Kapalua (p 78).

Best for **Families**
★ Kamaole III Beach Park, South
Kihei Rd., Kihei (p 79).

Best for **Hawaiian History &
Culture**
★ Waianapanapa State Park, MM 32
Hana Hwy. (Hwy. 360), Hana (p 82).

Longest **White-Sand Beach**
★★ Oneloa Beach (Big Beach),
South Makena Rd., Makena (p 80).

Best for **Kayaking**
★★ Maluaka Beach (Makena
Beach), Makena Rd., Makena (p 80),
and ★★★ Kapalua Beach, past MM
30 by Napali Kai Beach Resort,
Honoapiilani Rd., Kapalua (p 79).

Best for **Picnicking**
Wahikuli County Wayside Park,
MM 23, Honoapiilani Hwy. (Hwy. 30),
Lahaina (p 81).

Best **Protected Beach**
★★★ Kapalua Beach, past MM 30,
by Napali Kai Beach Resort,
Honoapiilani Rd., Kapalua (p 79).

Most **Romantic**
★★ Wailea Beach, fronting Four
Seasons Maui, and the Grand
Wailea Resort, Wailea Alanui Rd.,
Wailea (p 82).

Best for **People-Watching**
★★ Kaanapali Beach, Kaanapali
(p 79).

Safest for **Kids**
Launiupoko County Wayside Park,
MM 18, Honoapiilani Hwy. (Hwy. 30),
Lahaina (p 80).

Safest for **Swimming**
★ Kamaole III Beach Park, South
Kihei Rd., Kihei (p 79).

Best for **Shade**
★★ D. T. Fleming Beach Park,
Honoapiilani Hwy. (Hwy. 30),
Kapalua (p 78).

Best **for Snorkeling**
★★ Kaanapali Beach, fronting Sheraton Maui, Kaanapali (p 79).

Best for **Board Surfing**
★★ Hamoa Beach, Haneoo Rd.,
Hana (p 78).

Best **View**
★★ Maluaka Beach (Makena
Beach), Makena Rd., Makena (p 80).

Best for **Windsurfing**
★ Hookipa Beach Park, MM 9 Hana
Hwy. (Hwy. 36), Paia (p 78).

Best for **Sunbathing**
★★ Hamoa Beach, Haneoo Rd.,
Hana (p 78).

Baldwin Beach.

Maui Beaches A to Z

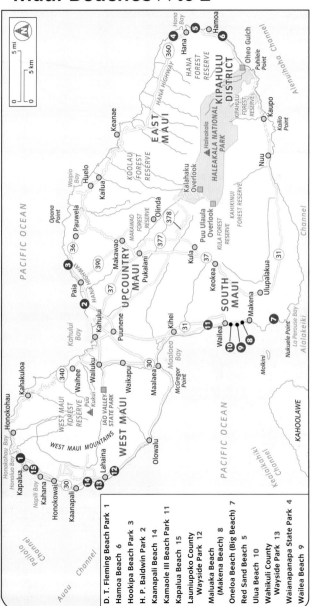

D. T. Fleming Beach Park 1
Hamoa Beach 6
Hookipa Beach Park 3
H. P. Baldwin Park 2
Kaanapali Beach 14
Kamaole III Beach Park 11
Kapalua Beach 15
Launiupoko County
Wayside Park 12
Maluaka Beach
(Makena Beach) 8
Oneloa Beach (Big Beach) 7
Red Sand Beach 5
Ulua Beach 10
Wahikuli County
Wayside Park 13
Waianapanapa State Park 4
Wailea Beach 9

Maui's Beautiful Beaches

Maui has more than 80 accessible beaches of every conceivable description, from rocky black-sand beauties to powdery golden ones. The ones I've described in this chapter represent my personal favorites, carefully chosen to suit a variety of needs, tastes, and interests. All beaches (even those in front of exclusive resorts) are public property, and you are welcome to visit. Hawaii state law requires all resorts and hotels to offer public right-of-way access to the beach, along with public parking. So don't be shy—just because a beach fronts a hotel doesn't mean that you can't enjoy the water.

★★ kids **D. T. Fleming Beach Park.** This quiet, out-of-the-way beach cove is a great place to take the family. The crescent-shaped beach, north of the Ritz-Carlton Hotel, is bordered by Ironwood trees, which provide shade on the land side. The waters are generally good for swimming and snorkeling. Facilities include restrooms, showers, picnic tables, barbecue grills, and a paved parking lot. *Past MM 30, Honoapiilani Hwy. (Hwy. 30), Kapalua.*

★★ **Hamoa Beach.** This half-moon-shaped, gray-sand beach (a mix of coral and lava) in a truly tropical setting is a favorite among sunbathers seeking rest and refuge. The Hotel Hana-Maui maintains the beach and acts as though it's private, which it isn't—so just march down the lava-rock steps and grab a spot on the sand. The 100-foot-(30m-) wide beach is three football fields long and sits below 30-foot (9m) black-lava sea cliffs. Hamoa is often swept by powerful rip currents. Surf breaks offshore and rolls ashore, making this a popular surfing and bodysurfing area. The calm left side is best for snorkeling in summer. The hotel has numerous facilities for guests; an outdoor shower and restrooms are available to non-guests. Parking is limited.

Haneoo Rd., off Hana Hwy. (Hwy. 360), Hana.

★ **Hookipa Beach Park.** Due to its constant winds and endless waves, Hookipa attracts top windsurfers and wave jumpers from around the globe. Surfers and fishermen also enjoy this small, gold-sand beach at the foot of a grassy cliff, which provides a natural amphitheater for spectators. Except when international competitions are being held, weekdays are the best time to watch the daredevils fly over the waves. When the water is flat, snorkelers and divers explore the reef. Facilities include restrooms,

Hamoa's gray-sand beach.

showers, pavilions, picnic tables, barbecue grills, and a parking lot. *Two miles past Paia, MM 9 Hana Hwy. (36), Paia.*

H. P. Baldwin Park. This beach park draws lots of Maui residents, especially body-board enthusiasts. The surf breaks along the entire length of the white sand, creating perfect conditions for body boarding. On occasion the waves get big enough for surfing. A couple of swimming areas are safe enough for children: one in the lee of the beach rocks near the large pavilion, and another at the opposite end of the beach, where beach rocks create a small protected area. Facilities include a large pavilion with picnic tables and kitchen facilities, barbecue grills, additional picnic tables on the grassy area, restrooms, showers, a semi-paved parking area, a baseball diamond, and a soccer field. The park is busy on weekends; weekdays are much quieter. *MM 6 Hana Hwy. (Hwy. 360), between Spreckelsville and Paia.*

★★ Kaanapali Beach. Four-mile-(6.4km-) long Kaanapali is one of Maui's best beaches, with grainy gold sand as far as the eye can see. Because Kaanapali is so long, and because most hotels have adjacent swimming pools, the beach is crowded only in pockets—you'll find plenty of spots to be alone. Summertime swimming is excellent. There's fabulous snorkeling around **Black Rock,** in front of the Sheraton. The water is clear, calm, and populated with clouds of tropical fish. You might even spot a turtle or two. Facilities consist of outdoor showers. Parking is a problem, though. *Look for Public Beach Access signs off Kaanapali Pkwy. (off Honoapiilani Hwy. 30, in the Kaanapali Resort.*

★ kids Kamaole III Beach Park. On weekends this beach is

Kamaole Beach Park.

jam-packed with fishermen, picnickers, swimmers, and snorkelers. But during the week "Kam-3," as locals call it, often empties out. This beach park features a playground for children and a grassy lawn that meets the sand. Swimming is safe, but scattered lava rocks are toe stubbers at the water line, and parents should watch to make sure that kids don't venture too far out, because the bottom slopes off quickly. Both the north and south shores are rocky fingers with a surge big enough to attract fish (and snorkelers to watch them), while winter waves attract bodysurfers. Facilities include restrooms, showers, picnic tables, barbecue grills, and lifeguards. *South Kihei Rd., across from Keonekai Rd., Kihei.*

★★★ Kapalua Beach. This is a postcard-perfect beach: a golden crescent bordered by two palm-studded points. Protected from strong winds and currents by lava-rock promontories, Kapalua's calm waters are great for snorkelers and swimmers of all ages and abilities, and the bay is big enough to paddle a kayak around without getting into the more challenging channel that

Kapalua Beach.

separates Maui from Molokai. Fish hang out by the rocks, making it great for snorkeling. Facilities include outdoor showers, restrooms, lifeguards, a rental shack, and plenty of shade. Parking is limited to about 30 spaces in a small lot. *Past MM 30, by Napali Kai Beach Resort, Honoapiilani Rd., Kapalua.*

kids Launiupoko County Wayside Park. Families with children will love this small, shady park with a large wading pool for kids and a small sandy beach with good swimming when conditions are right. The view from the park is one of the best, with the islands of Kahoolawe, Lanai, and Molokai in the distance. Facilities include a paved parking lot, restrooms, showers, picnic tables, and barbecue grills. It's crowded on weekends. *MM 18, Honoapiilani Hwy. (Hwy. 30), Lahaina.*

★★ Maluaka Beach (Makena Beach). This is the place for views: Molokini Crater and Kahoolawe are both visible in the distance. Maluaka itself is a short, wide, palm-fringed crescent of golden, grainy sand set between two black-lava points and bounded by big sand dunes topped by a grassy knoll. Swimming and kayaking in the mostly calm bay are first-rate. Facilities include restrooms, showers, a landscaped park, lifeguards, and roadside parking. *Along Makena Alanui, look for the shoreline access sign near the Makena Prince Hotel, turn right, and head down to the shore on Makena Rd., Makena.*

★★ Oneloa Beach (Big Beach). Oneloa ("long sand"), known as Big Beach, is 3,300-feet (990m) long and more than 100 feet (30m) wide. Mauians come here to swim, fish, sunbathe, surf, and enjoy the view of Kahoolawe and Lanai. Snorkeling is good around the north end at the foot of Puu Olai, a 360-foot (108m) cinder cone. During storms, however,

Makena Beach.

big waves lash the shore and a strong rip current sweeps the sharp drop-off, posing a danger for inexperienced open-ocean swimmers. On the other side of Puu Olai is **Little Beach,** a small pocket beach where assorted nudists work on their all-over tans (much to the chagrin of uptight authorities, who take a dim view of public nudity). You could get a sunburn in a sensitive spot and a lewd-conduct ticket, too. Facilities include portable toilets and parking. *South Makena Rd., Makena.*

Red Sand Beach. This beach on the ocean side of Kauiki Hill, just south of Hana Bay, is truly a sight to see. It's in a wild, natural setting on a pocket cove, where the volcanic cinder cone lost its seaward wall to erosion and spilled red cinders everywhere, creating the red sands. But before you put on your bathing suit, there are three things to know about this beach: You have to trespass to get here (which is against the law); it can be extremely dangerous due to heavy rains (there have been several serious injuries on the muddy, slippery terrain); and nudity (also illegal in Hawaii) is common here. If you are determined to go, ask for permission at the Hotel Hana-Maui. Also inquire about conditions on the trail (which drops several stories down to the ocean rocks). To reach the beach, put on solid walking shoes (no flip-flops) and walk south on Uakea Rd., past Haoli St. and the Hotel Hana-Maui, to the parking lot for the hotel's Sea Ranch Cottages. Turn left and cross the open field next to the Hana Community Center. Look for the dirt trail and follow it to the huge ironwood tree, where you turn right (do not go ahead to the old Japanese cemetery). Use the ironwood trees to maintain your balance as you follow the ever-eroding cinder footpath a short distance along the

Oneloa Beach.

shoreline, down the narrow cliff trail (do not attempt this if it's wet). The trail suddenly turns a corner, and into view comes the burnt-red beach, set off by the turquoise waters, black lava, and vivid green ironwood trees. The lava outcropping protects the bay and makes it safe for swimming. Snorkeling is excellent, and there's a natural whirlpool area on the Hana Bay side of the cove. Stay away from the surge area where the ocean enters the cove.

★ **Ulua Beach.** One of the most popular beaches in Wailea, Ulua is a long, wide, crescent-shaped gold-sand beach between two rocky points. When the ocean is calm, Ulua offers Wailea's best snorkeling; when it's rough, the waves are excellent for bodysurfers. Crowded conditions make it perfect for meeting people. Facilities include showers and restrooms. *Look for the blue shoreline access sign, on Wailea Alanui Dr., Wailea.*

Wahikuli County Wayside Park. This small stretch of beach is one of Lahaina's most popular beach parks. It's packed on weekends, but during the week it's a

Wailea Beach.

great place for swimming, snorkeling, sunbathing, and picnics. Facilities include paved parking, restrooms, showers, and small covered pavilions with picnic tables and barbecue grills. *MM 23, Honoapiilani Hwy. (Hwy. 30), between Lahaina and Kaanapali.*

★ **Waianapanapa State Park.** This 120-acre beach park is a wonderful area for both shoreline hikes (mosquitoes are plentiful, so bring insect repellent) and picnicking. Swimming is generally unsafe due to powerful rip currents and strong waves breaking offshore, which roll into the beach unchecked. Waianapanapa is crowded on weekends; weekdays are generally a better bet. Facilities include 12 cabins, a beach park, picnic tables, barbecue grills, restrooms, showers, a parking lot, a shoreline hiking trail, and a black-sand beach. *MM 32 Hana Hwy. (Hwy. 360), Hana. See p 90.*

★★ **Wailea Beach.** From the beach, the view out to sea is magnificent, framed by neighboring Kahoolawe and Lanai and the tiny crescent of Molokini. Grab your sweetie at sunset and watch the clear waters tumble to shore; this is as romantic as it gets. Facilities include restrooms, outdoor showers, and limited free parking. *Look for the blue shoreline access sign, on Wailea Alanui Dr., Wailea.* ●

The Legend of Waianapanapa

Waianapanapa Park gets its name from the legend of the Waianapanapa Cave. Chief Kaakea, a jealous and cruel man, suspected his wife, Popoalaea, of having an affair. Popoalaea left her husband and hid herself in a chamber of the Waianapanapa Cave. A few days later, when Kaakea was passing by the cave, the shadow of a servant gave away Popoalaea's hiding place, and Kaakea killed her. During certain times of the year, the water in the tide pool turns red as a tribute to Popoalaea, commemorating her death. (Killjoy scientists claim, however, that the change in color is due to the presence of small red shrimp.)

6 The Great **Outdoors**

Haleakala National Park

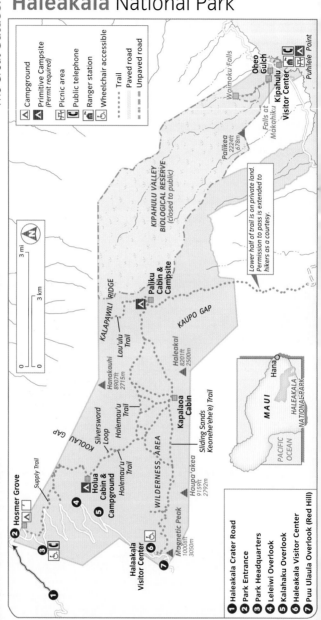

Legend:
- △ Campground
- ◢ Primitive Campsite (Permit required)
- 🏕 Picnic area
- ☎ Public telephone
- 🏠 Ranger station
- ♿ Wheelchair accessible
- ········· Trail
- ——— Paved road
- ▬ ▬ ▬ Unpaved road

0 — 3 mi
0 — 3 km

Hosmer Grove

Supply Trail

KOOLAU GAP

Silversword Loop

Halemau'u Trail

Halemau'u Trail

Holua Cabin & Campground

Hanakauhi 8907ft 2715m

KALAPAWILI RIDGE

Lau'ulu Trail

Paliku Cabin & Campsite

KAUPO GAP

Haleakal 8201ft 2500m

KIPAHULU VALLEY BIOLOGICAL RESERVE (closed to public)

Palikea 2224ft 678m

Waimoku Falls

Oheo Gulch

Kipahulu Visitor Center

Puhilele Point

Falls at Makahiku

Lower half of trail is on private land. Permission to pass is extended to hikers as a courtesy.

Kapalaoa Cabin

Sliding Sands (Keonehe'ehe') Trail

WILDERNESS AREA

Haupa'akea 9159ft 2792m

Magnetic Peak 10008ft 3050m

Haleakala Visitor Center

MAUI
Hana
PACIFIC OCEAN
HALEAKALA NATIONAL PARK

1. Haleakala Crater Road
2. Park Entrance
3. Park Headquarters
4. Leleiwi Overlook
5. Kalahaku Overlook
6. Haleakala Visitor Center
7. Puu Ulaula Overlook (Red Hill)

At once forbidding and compelling, Haleakala ("house of the sun") National Park is Maui's most compelling natural attraction. More than 1.3 million people a year ascend the 10,023-foot- (3,007m-) high mountain to peer into the crater of the world's largest dormant volcano. The crater is large enough that the entire island of Manhattan would fit inside: 3,000-feet (900m) deep, 7½-miles (12.1km) long by 2½-miles (4km) wide, and encompassing 19 square miles (49.2km sq.). But there's more to do here than simply stare in a big black hole: Just going up the mountain is an experience in itself. The snaky road passes through big, puffy, cumulus clouds, climbing from sea level to 10,000 feet (3,000m) in just 37 miles (59.6km) to offer magnificent views of the isthmus of Maui, the West Maui Mountains, and the Pacific Ocean. START: **Kahului. Trip length: 37 miles (59.6km); about a 2-hour drive**

Travel Tips

Pukalani is the last town for water, food, and gas (there are no facilities beyond the ranger stations). On the way back down, put your car in low gear so you won't destroy your brakes on the descent.

From Kahului, take Hwy. 37 to Hwy. 377 to Hwy. 378.

❶ ★★★ **Haleakala Crater Road.** If you look on a Maui map, there's a black wiggly line that looks like this: WWWWW. That's Hwy. 378, also known as Haleakala Crater Road—one of the fastest-ascending roads in the world. This grand corniche has at least 33 switchbacks; passes through numerous climate zones; goes under, in, and out of clouds; takes you past rare silversword plants and endangered Hawaiian geese sailing through the clear, thin air; and offers a view that extends for more than 100 miles (30km). Along the way, expect fog, rain, and wind. You might also encounter stray cattle and downhill bicyclists.

❷ **Park Entrance.** A ranger will collect the entrance fee of $10 per car (or $2 for a bicycle), good for a week of unlimited entry.

❸ **Park Headquarters.** Here you can pick up information on park programs and activities and get camping permits. Restrooms, a pay phone, and drinking water are available. Don't miss my favorite Haleakala native, Hawaii's endangered **nene,** or Hawaiian goose. With its black face, buff cheeks, and partially webbed feet, the gray-brown bird looks like a small Canada goose with zebra stripes; it brays out "nay-nay" (hence its name), doesn't migrate, and prefers lava beds to lakes. The unusual goose clings to a precarious existence on these

Hawaii's endangered nene.

Before You Go

At the 10,023-foot (3,007m) summit of Haleakala National Park, weather changes fast. With wind chill, temperatures can drop below freezing any time of year. Summers are usually dry and warm; winters wet, windy, and cold. Before you go, get current weather conditions from the park (☎ 808/572-4400) or the **National Weather Service** (☎ 808/871-5054). Bring water and a jacket or a blanket, especially if you go up for sunrise. (Sunsets at the summit are also spectacular.)

As you ascend the slopes, the temperature drops about 3°F (2°C) every 1,000 feet (300m), so the top can be 30°F (16°C) cooler than it was at sea level. Come prepared with sweaters, jackets, and rain gear.

From sunrise to noon, the light is weak, but the view is usually cloud-free. The best time for photos is in the afternoon, when the sun lights the crater and clouds are sparse. Full-moon nights also make for spectacular viewing.

alpine slopes. Vast populations of more than 25,000 once inhabited Hawaii, but predation coupled with habitat destruction have nearly caused its extinction. By 1951 there were only 30 left. Now protected as Hawaii's state bird, the wild nene on Haleakala number fewer than 250. ☎ 808/572-4400; www.nps.gov/hale. Daily from 7am–4pm.

❹ ★ Leleiwi Overlook. Just beyond MM 17, pull into the parking area. From here a short trail leads

Bikers admiring the view from Kalahaku Overlook.

A rare silversword.

you to a panoramic view of the lunarlike crater. When the clouds are low and the sun is in the right place, usually around sunset, you can experience a phenomenon known as the "Specter of the Brocken"— you can see a reflection of your shadow, ringed by a rainbow, in the clouds below. It's an optical illusion caused by a rare combination of sun, shadow, and fog that occurs only in three places on the planet: Haleakala, Scotland, and Germany.

⑤ ★ Kalahaku Overlook. This is the best place to see a rare **silversword.** Looking like something from outer-space, its silvery bayonets display tiny purple bouquets—like a spacey artichoke with attitude. This botanical wonder proved irresistible to collectors, who gathered them in

gunnysacks for Chinese potions, for British specimen collections, and just for the sheer thrill of having something so unusual. Silverswords grow only in Hawaii, take from 4 to 50 years to bloom, and then, usually between May and October, send up a 1- to 6-foot (.3–1.8m) stalk with a purple bouquet of sunflower-like blooms.

⑥ ★ Haleakala Visitor Center. Just before the summit, this small building offers a panoramic view of the volcanic landscape, with photos identifying the various features and exhibits that explain its history, ecology, geology, and volcanology. Park staff are often on hand to answer questions. The only facilities are restrooms and water. Rangers offer excellent, informative, and free **naturalist talks** at 9:30, 10:30, and 11:30am daily in the summit building, and lead guided hikes from here. *Near the summit, 11 miles (17.7km) from the park entrance. P.O. Box 369, Makawao, HI 96768.* ☎ *808/572-4400; www.nps.gov/ hale. Daily from sunrise–3pm.*

⑦ ★ Puu Ulaula Overlook (Red Hill). This is it—the volcano's highest point—you'll feel as if you're at the edge of the earth. You'll also notice a mysterious cluster of buildings officially known as Haleakala Observatories, but unofficially called **Science City.** If you're here at sunrise, the building at Puu Ulaula Overlook, a triangle of glass that serves as a windbreak, is the best viewing spot. After the daily miracle of sunrise—the sun seems to rise out of the vast crater (hence the name "House of the Sun")—you can see all the way across Alenuihaha Channel to the often snowcapped summit of Mauna Kea on the Big Island.

Maui's Best Hiking & Camping

Haleakala National Park

- 378
- ❷ Park Headquarters
- Leleiwi Overlook
- ❸
- Kalahaku Overlook
- ❹ *Hanakauhi*
- KALAPAWILI RIDGE
- KIPAHULU VALLEY BIOLOGICAL RESERVE (closed to public)
- WILDERNESS AREA
- ❻
- *Magnetic Peak*
- ❺
- *Haupa'akea* *Haleakal*
- KAUPO GAP
- ❶
- *Waimoku Falls*
- *Palikea*
- Oheo Gulch
- *Falls at Makahiku*
- Puhilele Point

0 — 3 mi
0 — 3 km
N

- Kapalua
- 30
- 340
- PACIFIC OCEAN
- ❿
- 36
- Lahaina
- WEST MAUI Wailuku
- 30
- Kahului
- UPCOUNTRY MAUI
- *Auau Channel*
- 30
- 360
- ❼
- EAST MAUI
- ❽
- Hana
- 377
- 378
- MAUI
- 31
- HALEAKALA NATIONAL PARK
- KIPAHULU DISTRICT
- Wailea
- ❾
- SOUTH MAUI
- 31
- *Kealaikahiki Channel*
- Area map above

- MAUI
- PACIFIC OCEAN
- Hana
- HALEAKALA NATIONAL PARK

Cabin Camping in Haleakala National Park

Holua 3
Kapalaoa 5
Paliku 6

Hiking

Haleakala National Park: Halemauu Trail 4
Haleakala National Park: Sliding Sands Trail 1
Keanae Arboretum 7
Polipoli State Park 9
Waianapanapa State Park 8

Camping

Haleakala National Park: Holua 3
Haleakala National Park: Hosmer Grove 2
Haleakala National Park: Paliku 6
Kanaha Beach Park 10
Polipoli State Park 9
Waianapanapa State Park 8

In the past 3 decades, Maui has grown from a rural island to a fast-paced resort destination, but its natural beauty largely remains; there are still many places that can be explored only on foot. Bring your own gear, as there are no places to rent camping equipment on Maui.

Haleakala National Park

★★★ **Hiking.** Hiking into Maui's dormant volcano is the best way to see it. The terrain inside the wilderness area of the volcano, which ranges from burnt-red cinder cones to ebony-black lava flows, is simply spectacular. Inside the crater are some 27 miles (43.5km) of hiking trails, two camping sites, and three cabins. The best route takes in two trails: you head into the crater along **Sliding Sands Trail,** which begins on the rim at 9,800 feet (2,940m) and descends to the valley floor at 6,600 feet (1,980m), and back out along **Halemauu Trail.** The 11-mile (17.7km) one-way descent takes 9 hours. For more information on visiting Haleakala, see p 85. *To get to the summit from Kahului, take Hwy. 37 to Hwy. 377 to Hwy. 378.* ☎ *808/ 572-4400; www.nps.gov/hale.*

Camping. Hosmer Grove, at 6,800 feet (2,040m), is a small, open grassy area surrounded by a forest near the entrance to Haleakala National Park. This is the best place to spend the night in a tent if you

want to see the Haleakala sunrise. No permits are needed at Hosmer Grove, and there's no charge—but you can stay for only 3 nights (just 2 of those consecutive) during a 30-day period. The two tent-camping areas inside the volcano are **Holua,** just off Halemauu at 6,920 feet (1,887m); and **Paliku,** just before the Kaupo Gap at the eastern end of the valley, at 6,380 feet (1,914m). Facilities at both campgrounds are limited to pit toilets and nonpotable catchment water. Permits are issued daily at park headquarters on a first-come, first-served basis.

Cabin Camping. The three cabins inside the crater are spaced so that each is an easy walk from the previous one: **Holua** cabin is on the Halemauu Trail, **Kapalaoa** cabin is on the Sliding Sands Trail, and **Paliku** cabin is on the eastern end by the Kaupo Gap. Each has 12 padded bunks (but no bedding; bring your own), a table, chairs, cooking utensils, a two-burner propane stove, and a wood-burning stove with firewood (you might also have a few

Hiking in Haleakala.

Getting a Camping Permit

All campers on Maui must have a permit. The requirements vary, and it does take time and effort to get a permit. Depending on where you're headed (see write-ups below), the following places issue permits: **Haleakala National Park,** P.O. Box 369, Makawao, HI 96768 (☎ 808/572-4400; www.nps.gov/hale); **Hawaii State Department of Land and Natural Resources,** State Parks Division, P.O. Box 621, Honolulu, HI 96809 (☎ 808/587-0300; www.state.hi.us/dlnr); **Maui County Parks and Recreation,** 1580-C Kaahumanu Ave., Wailuku, HI 96793 (☎ 808/243-7380; www.mauimapp.com).

cockroaches). The rates are $55 a night for groups of one to six. The cabins are so popular that the National Park Service has a lottery system for reservations. Requests for cabins must be made 3 months in advance. You're limited to no more than 2 nights in one cabin and no more than 3 nights within the wilderness per month.

Kanaha Beach Park

Camping. This popular county park has two separate areas for camping: 7 tent sites on the beach and an additional 10 tent sites inland. The park is a favorite of windsurfers, who take advantage of the strong winds that roar across this end of the island. Facilities include a paved parking lot, portable toilets, outdoor showers, barbecue grills, and picnic tables. Camping is limited to 3 consecutive days; the permit fee is $3 per adult and 50¢ for children, per night, and can be obtained from the Maui County Parks and Recreation Department, see box above. *On Ala-hao St. in Kahalui, just west of the Kahului Airport.*

Keanae Arboretum

Hiking. This easy 2-mile (3.2km), family-friendly walk through the

Keanae Arboretum, passes through a forest with both native and introduced plants. Allow 1 to 2 hours, longer if you want to swim. Bring rain gear and mosquito repellent. *47 miles (75.7km) from Kahului, along the Hana Hwy.*

Polipoli State Park

★ **Hiking & Camping.** At 5,300 to 6,200 feet (1,590m–1,860m), and part of the 21,000-acre (8,400 hectare) Kula and Kahikinui Forest Reserve on the slope of Haleakala, Polipoli doesn't seem like your typical image of Hawaii (it's downright cold at 6,200 feet/1,860m!) But there's great hiking on the **Polipoli Loop,** an easy, 5-mile (8km) hike that takes about 3 hours and branches out to a variety of longer trails. Dress warmly to meander through groves of eucalyptus, swamp mahogany, and hybrid cypress. Camping is allowed in the park with a $5-per-night permit from the Division of State Parks, see box above. *Take Hwy. 37 to Keokea and turn right on Hwy. 337; after less than ½ mile (0.8km) turn on Waipoli Rd. and continue for 10 miles (16km) to the park.*

Waianapanapa State Park

★★★ **Hiking & Camping.** Tucked in a tropical jungle, on the outskirts

Waianapanapa State Park.

with camping and hiking. The **coastal trail** is an easy, 6-mile (9.7km) hike that parallels the sea, traveling past lava cliffs and a forest of lauhala trees. Allow 4 hours for the hike. The best time of day is either the early morning or the late evening, when the light on the lava and surf makes for great photos. The park has 12 cabins and a tent campground. Go for the cabins, as it rains torrentially here, sometimes turning the campground into something like a mud-wrestling arena. Tent-camping is $5 per night but limited to 5 nights in a 30-day period. Permits are available from the State Parks Division, see box on p 90. *Just after MM32, turn off the Hana Hwy. (Hwy.360) at the Waianapanapa State Park sign. Continue down Waianapanapa Rd. to the end.*

of the little coastal town of Hana, is Waianapanapa State Park, a black-sand beach set in an emerald forest,

Safe Hiking & Camping

Water might be everywhere in Hawaii, but more than likely it isn't safe to drink. Most stream water must be treated because cattle, pigs, and goats have contaminated the water upstream. The Department of Health continually warns campers of *bacterium leptospirosis,* which is found in freshwater streams throughout the state and enters the body through breaks in the skin or through the mucous membranes. It produces flu-like symptoms and can be fatal. Firewood isn't always available, so it's a good idea to carry a small, light, backpacking stove, which you can use both to boil water and to cook meals. Make sure that your drinking water is safe by vigorously boiling it, or if boiling is not an option, use tablets with hydroperiodide; portable water filters will not screen out *bacterium leptospirosis.*

Remember, Maui is not crime-free: Never leave your valuables unprotected. Carry a day pack if you have a campsite, and never camp alone.

Some more do's and don'ts: Do bury personal waste away from streams, don't eat unknown fruit, do carry your trash out, and don't forget there is very little twilight in Maui when the sun sets—it gets dark quickly.

Maui's Best Golf Courses

Elleair Maui Golf Club 3
Kaanapali Courses 2
Kapalua Resort Courses 1
Makena Courses 5
Waiehu Municipal Golf Course 6
Wailea Courses 4

In some circles, Maui is synonymous with golf. The island's world-famous courses start at the northern tip of the island and roll right around to Kaanapali, jumping down to Kihei and Wailea in the south. First-time Maui golfers should know that it's windy here, especially between 10am and 2pm, when winds of 10 to 15 mph are the norm. Play two to three clubs up or down to compensate. I also recommend bringing extra balls—the rough is thicker here and the wind will pick your ball up and drop it in very unappealing places (like water hazards).

Renting Golf Gear

Golf Club Rentals (☎ 808/665-0800; www.mauiclubrentals.com) has custom-built clubs for men, women, and juniors (right- and left-handed), which can be delivered island-wide; rates are $20 to $25 a day.

Elleair Maui Golf Club (formerly Silversword Golf Club). Sitting in the foothills of Haleakala, just high enough to afford spectacular ocean vistas from every hole, this is a course for golfers who love the views as much as the fairways and the greens. It's very forgiving. *Just one caveat:* Go in the morning. Not only is it cooler, but more important, it's also less windy. In the afternoon the winds bluster down Haleakala with great gusto. Facilities include a clubhouse, driving range, putting green, pro shop, and lessons. *1345 Piilani Hwy. (near Lipoa St. turnoff), Kihei. ☎ 808/874-0777; www.golf-maui.com. Greens fees: $105; twilight rate $80.*

★ Kaanapali Courses. The courses at Kaanapali offer a challenge to all golfers, from high handicappers to near-pros. The par-72, 6,305-yard **North Course** is a true Robert Trent Jones, Sr., design: an abundance of wide bunkers; several long, stretched-out tees; and the largest, most contoured greens on Maui. The par-72, 6,250-yard **South**

Course is an Arthur Jack Snyder design. Although shorter than the North Course, it requires more accuracy on the narrow, hilly fairways. Facilities include a driving range, putting course, and clubhouse with dining. You'll have a better chance of getting a tee time on weekdays. *Off Hwy. 30, Kaanapali. ☎ 808/661-3691; www.kaanapali-golf.com. Greens fees: $180 (North Course), $140 (South Course); Kaanapali guests pay $145 (North), $115 (South); twilight rates $85 (North), $75 (South) for everyone. At the first stoplight in Kaanapali, turn onto Kaanapali Pkwy.; the first building on your right is the clubhouse.*

★★★ Kapalua Resort Courses. The views from these three championship courses are worth the greens fees alone. The par-72, 6,761-yard **Bay Course** (☎ 808/669-8820) was designed by Arnold Palmer and Ed Seay. This course is a bit forgiving, with its wide fairways; the greens, however, are difficult to read. The par-71, 6,632-yard **Village Course** (☎ 808/669-8830), another Palmer/Seay design, is the most scenic of the three courses here. The **Plantation Course** (☎ 808/669-8877), site of the Mercedes Championships, is a Ben Crenshaw/Bill Coore design. This 6,547-yard, par-73 course, set on a rolling hillside, is excellent for developing your low shots and precise chipping. Facilities for all three courses include locker rooms, a driving range, and a good restaurant. Weekdays are your best bet for tee times. *Off Hwy. 30, Kapalua.* ☎ *877/KAPALUA; www. kapaluamaui.com. Greens fees: $185 ($130 for hotel guests) Village Course ($85 twilight rate); $200 ($140 for guests) Bay Course ($90 twilight rate); $250 ($160 for guests) Plantation Course ($100 twilight rate).*

★★ **Makena Courses.** Here you'll find 36 holes of "Mr. Hawaii Golf"—Robert Trent Jones, Jr.—at his best. Add to that some spectacular views: Molokini islet looms in the background, humpback whales gambol offshore in winter, and the tropical sunsets are spectacular. The par-72, 6,876-yard **South Course** has a couple of holes you'll never forget. The par-72, 6,823-yard **North Course** is more difficult and more spectacular. Facilities include a clubhouse, a driving range, two putting greens, a pro shop, lockers, and lessons. Beware of weekend crowds. *On Makena Alanui Dr., just past the Maui Prince Hotel.* ☎ *808/ 879-3344; www.maui.net/~makena. Greens fees: North Course $185 ($110 for Makena Resort guests), twilight rate $125 ($95 for guests);*

Makena golf courses.

South Course $185 ($110 for resort guests), twilight rate $125 ($95 for guests); guest rates vary seasonally, with higher rates in the winter.

Waiehu Municipal Golf Course. This public, oceanside, par-72 golf course is like two courses in one: The first 9 holes, built in 1930, are set along the dramatic coastline, while the back 9 holes, added in 1966, head toward the mountains. It's a fun course that probably won't challenge your handicap. The only hazard here is the wind, which can rip off the ocean and play havoc with your ball. Facilities include a snack bar, driving range, practice greens, golf-club rental, and clubhouse. Because this is a public course, the greens fees are low—but getting a tee time is tough. *P.O. Box 507, Wailuku, HI 96793.* ☎ *808/244-5934; www.co. maui.hi.us/parks/maui/central/ WaiehuGolfCourse.htm. Greens fees $40 Mon–Fri, $45 Sat–Sun and holidays. From the Kahului Airport, turn right on the Hana Hwy. (Hwy. 36), which becomes Kaahumanu Ave. (Hwy. 32). Turn right at the stoplight at the junction of Waiehu Beach Rd. (Hwy. 340). Go another 1½ miles (2.4km), and you'll see the entrance on your right.*

Golf Tips

If you're trying to get a tee time at a public course, keep in mind that weekdays are always better than weekends, when the locals flood the field. You'll have better luck teeing off after 9am, and afternoons generally are wide open. And, of course, book in advance, as soon as you have your travel dates.

★★ **Wailea Courses.** You can choose among three courses at Wailea. The **Blue Course**, a par-72,

One of Wailea's golf courses.

6,758-yard course designed by Arthur Jack Snyder and dotted with bunkers and water hazards, is for duffers and pros alike. A little more difficult is the par-72, 7,078-yard championship **Gold Course,** with narrow fairways, several tricky dog-leg holes, and natural hazards like lava-rock walls. The **Emerald Course,** which like the Gold Course was designed by Robert Trent Jones, Jr., is Wailea's newest, with tropical landscaping and a player-friendly design. With 54 holes to play, getting a tee time is slightly easier on weekends than at other resorts, but weekdays are still the best (the Emerald Course is usually the toughest to book). Facilities include two pro shops, restaurants, locker rooms, and a complete golf training facility. *Wailea Alanui Dr. (off Wailea Iki Dr.), Wailea.* 📞 *888/328-MAUI or 808/875-7450; www.wailea golf.com. Greens fees: Blue Course $160 ($125–$135 resort guests); Gold Course $190 ($160 resort guests); Emerald Course $190 ($160 resort guests).*

Golfing on a Budget

If your heart is set on playing on a resort course, book at least a week in advance. Ardent golfers on a budget should play in the afternoon, when discounted twilight rates are in effect. There's no guarantee you'll get 18 holes in, especially in winter when it's dark by 6pm, but you'll have an opportunity to experience these world-famous courses at half the usual fee.

For last-minute and discount tee times, call **Stand-by Golf** (📞 888/645-BOOK or 808/874-0600; www.stand-bygolf.com) between 7am and 9pm. Stand-by offers discounted (up to 50% off greens fees), guaranteed tee times for same-day or next-day golfing.

Adventures on Land

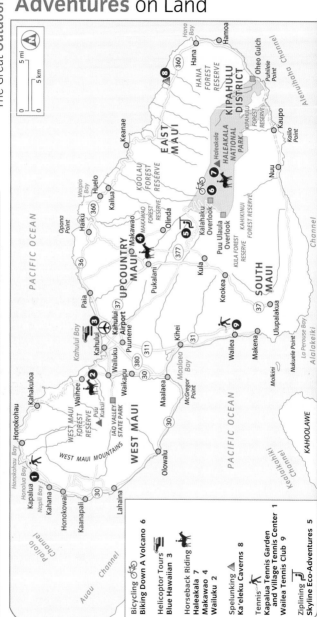

Bicycling
Biking Down A Volcano 6

Helicopter Tours
Blue Hawaiian 3

Horseback Riding
Haleakala 7
Makawao 4
Wailuku 2

Spelunking
Ka'eleku Caverns 8

Tennis
Kapalua Tennis Garden
and Village Tennis Center 1
Wailea Tennis Club 9

Ziplining
Skyline Eco-Adventures 5

Maui is known for its crystal-clear waters, but you'll also discover plenty of land-based adventures to enjoy. Haleakala is perfect for bicycling and horseback riding, the warm, sunny days are terrific for tennis, and real daredevils can try ziplining.

Bicycling

Biking Down a Volcano. It's not even close to dawn, but here you are, rubbing your eyes awake, riding in a van up the long, dark road to the top of Maui's sleeping volcano. It's colder than you ever thought possible for a tropical island. The air is thin. You stomp your chilly feet while you wait, sipping hot coffee. Then comes the sun, exploding over yawning Haleakala Crater—it's a mystical moment you won't soon forget. But there's no time to linger: Decked out in your screaming yellow jacket, you mount your steed and test its most important feature, the brakes, because you're about to coast 37 miles (59.6km) down a 10,000-foot (3,000m) volcano. All rates include hotel pickup, transport to the top, bicycle, safety equipment, and

meals. Wear layers of warm clothing—there may be a 30°F (17°C) change in temperature from the top of the mountain to the ocean. Generally, the tour groups will not take riders under 12, but younger children can ride along in the van that accompanies the groups. Pregnant women should also ride in the van. My pick for cruising down Haleakala is Maui's oldest downhill company, **Maui Downhill,** which offers a sunrise safari bike tour, including continental breakfast and brunch. *199 Dairy Rd., Kahului.* ☎ *800/535-BIKE or 808/871-2155; www.mauidownhill.com. From $125.*

Helicopter Flights

★★★ **Maui from the Air.** Only a helicopter can bring you face-to-face with remote sites like Maui's

Biking on Haleakala.

little-known Wall of Tears, near the summit of Puu Kukui in the West Maui Mountains. You'll glide through canyons etched with 1,000-foot (300m) waterfalls and over dense rainforests; you'll climb to 10,000 feet (3,000m), high enough to glimpse the summit of Haleakala, and fly by the dramatic vistas at Molokai. **Blue Hawaiian's** pilots are part Hawaiian historian, part DJ, part tour guide, and part amusement-ride operator. As you soar through the clouds, you'll learn about the island's flora, fauna, history, and culture. Blue Hawaiian is also the only helicopter company in the state to have the latest, high-tech, environmentally friendly (and quiet) Eco-Star helicopter. *Kahului Airport (☎ 800/745-BLUE or 808/871-8844; www.bluehawaiian.com). Flights vary from 30–100 minutes and range from $137–$303.*

Horseback Riding
Haleakala. If you'd like to ride down into Haleakala's crater, contact **Pony Express Tours,** which offers a variety of rides down to the crater floor and back up, and shorter 1- and 2-hour rides at Haleakala Ranch. *Hwy. 378, Kula.* ☎ *808/667-2200 or 808/878-6698; www.ponyexpresstours.com. Crater rides from $165.*

Makawao. Maui has spectacular adventure rides through rugged ranch lands, into tropical forests, and to remote swimming holes. My favorite is **Piiholo Ranch,** in Makawao. A working cattle ranch, owned by the *kamaaina* (longtime resident) Baldwin family, this is a horseback-riding adventure with a variety of rides to suit different abilities, from the morning picnic ride, a 3½-hour ride on the ranch, with a picnic lunch; to private rides, including working with the cowboys to round up the cattle. *Waiahiwi Rd., Makawao.* ☎ *866/572-5544 or 808/*

Horseback riding in Haleakala's crater.

357-5544; www.piiholo.com. Rides start at $160.

Wailuku. For an "out west" type of adventure, I like **Mendes Ranch & Trail Rides.** The 300-acre (120 hectares) Mendes Ranch is a real-life working cowboy ranch that has all the essential elements of an earthly paradise—rainbows, waterfalls, palm trees, coral-sand beaches, lagoons, tide pools, a rainforest, and its own volcanic peak (more than a mile high). Allan Mendes, a third-generation wrangler, will take you from the edge of the rainforest out to the sea. On the way, you'll cross tree-studded meadows where Texas longhorns sit in the shade and pass a dusty corral where Allan's father, Ernest, a champion roper, may be breaking in a wild horse. Allan keeps close watch, turning often in his saddle to make sure everyone is happy. He points out flora and fauna and fields questions, but generally just lets you soak up Maui's natural splendor in golden silence. My favorite is the morning ride, which lasts 2 hours and ends with a barbecue back at the corral. *3530 Kahekili Hwy., 5 miles (8km) past Wailuku.* ☎ *808/244-7320; www.mendesranch.com. $110.*

Spelunking

★ **Ka'eleku Caverns.** Don't miss the opportunity to see how the Hawaiian Islands were made by exploring a million-year-old underground lava tube/cave. Chuck Thorne, of **Maui Cave Adventures,** offers a look at this unique geological feature. After more than 10 years of leading scuba tours through underwater caves around Hawaii, Chuck discovered some caves on land. When the land surrounding the largest cave on Maui went on the market in 1996, Chuck snapped it up and started his own tour company. The self-guided tours take 30- to 45-minutes. *Ulaino Rd. just north of Hana.* ☎ *808/248-7308; www.mauicave.com. Saturdays between 10:30am–3:30pm. $12. Ages 6 and up.*

Tennis

★★★ **Kapalua Tennis Garden and Village Tennis Center.** Opened in 1979, the Tennis Garden has 10 Plexi-Pave courts paired in tiered clusters, with 4 lit for night play and surrounded by lush tropical foliage. Each set of courts is secluded in landscaped privacy with its own viewing lanai. Also available: private lessons, stroke-of-the-day clinics, drop-in clinics, and tournaments. The staff will match you up with a partner if you need one. *Kapalua Resort.* ☎ *808/669-5677; www.kapaluamaui.com. Court rentals are $14 per person for resort guests and $16 per person for nonguests.*

★★ **Wailea Tennis Club.** One of Maui's best facilities for playing the game, this resort club features: 11 Plexi-Pave courts (3 nighttime courts), backboard or wall, pro-shop, six USPTA pros available for lessons, and three doubles clinics a week. *131 Wailea Iki Pl., Wailea.* ☎ *808/879-1958; www.waileatennis.com. Court fees are $15 per player.*

Ziplining

Zipline Haleakala Tour. For those looking for a different perspective on Haleakala, **Skyline Eco-Adventures** blends a short hike through a eucalyptus forest with four "zipline" crossings. During the zipline crossing, you'll be outfitted with a seat harness and connected to a cable, then launched from a 70-foot- (21m-) high platform to "zip" along the cable suspended over the slopes of Haleakala. From this viewpoint, you fly over treetops, valleys, gulches, and waterfalls at 10 to 35 mph. These bird's-eye tours operate daily and take riders ages 12 and up, weighing between 80 and 300 pounds. *P.O. Box 880518, Pukalani, HI 96788. Take Hwy. 37 to Hwy. 377. Turn left on Hwy. 378 for 2.5 miles (4km).* ☎ *808/878-8400; www.sky linehawaii.com. $79 ($67 if you book online).*

Ziplining.

Maui's Best Snorkeling

| 0 | | 5 mi |
| 0 | | 5 km |

Honokohau Bay

Lipoa Point
Honolua Bay
Nakalele Point

Kapalua ❶ Honokahua
Honokohau

Kahakuloa Head

PACIFIC OCEAN

Napili
Bay
Kapalua
Beach
Kahana
Honokowai

Kahakuloa

Hakuhee Point

WEST MAUI
FOREST
RESERVE

WEST MAUI
MOUNTAINS

Waihee Point

Kaanapali

Kaanapali
Beach ❷

Waihee   Kahului Bay

Kanaha
Beach Park

Puu Kukui

Lahaina

Wailuku   Kahului

Kahului
Airport

IAO VALLEY
STATE PARK

WEST MAUI

Waikapu

Puunene

Honoapiilani Hwy.

Kuihelani Hwy.

Mokulele Hwy.

Auau

Channel

Olowalu ❸

Maui Ocean
Center

Maalaea

Papawai
Point

Maalaea
Bay   Kihei

Piilani Hwy.

PACIFIC
OCEAN

Kamaole Beach Parks

Kihei Rd.

❹

Wailea Beach

Wailea

Mokapu
& Ulua Beaches

❺

SOUTH
MAUI

Kealaikahiki
Channel

Maluaka (Makena) Beach

❻

Oneloa Beach (Big Beach)

Makena

Puu Olai

Ulupalakua

❼

Molkini

Kanahena

Nukuele
Point

Keoneoio

Molokini

La Perouse Bay

❽

Cape
Hanamanioa

KAHOOLAWE

Alalakeiki
Channel

Ahihi-Kinau Natural Preserve 8
Black Rock 2
Kamaole III Beach Park 4
Kapalua Beach 1
Makena Landing 6
Molokini 7
Olowalu 3
Ulua Beach 5

S norkeling is the main attraction in Maui—and almost any-
one can do it. All you need are a mask, a snorkel, fins, and some
basic swimming skills. Floating over underwater worlds through colorful clouds of tropical fish is like a dream. If you've never snorkeled
before, most resorts and excursion boats offer instruction, but it's
plenty easy to figure it out for yourself: In many places all you have
to do is wade into the water and look down. Below are my favorite
snorkeling spots in Maui.

★ **Ahihi-Kinau Natural Preserve.** Ahihi Bay is a 2,000-acre
(809–hectare) state natural area
reserve in the lee of Cape Kinau, on
Maui's rugged south coast, where
Haleakala's red-hot lava ran to the
sea in 1790. Fishing is strictly *kapu*
(forbidden) here, and the fish know
it; they're everywhere in this series
of rocky coves and black-lava tide
pools. The black, barren, lunarlike
land stands in stark contrast to the
green-blue water. After you snorkel,
check out La Pérouse Bay on the
south side of Cape Kinau, where the
French admiral La Pérouse became
the first European to set foot on
Maui. *Drive south on Makena on
Makena Alanui Rd.*

★★ **Black Rock.** In the Kaanapali
Beach Resort, in front of the Sheraton Hotel, Black Rock not only has
clear, calm water, but it's also populated with clouds of tropical fish.
You might even spot a turtle or two.
The third plus for this area is that all
the hotels and condominiums lining
the ocean here have swimming
pools, which means fewer swimmers in the water. *Look for Public
Beach Access signs off Kaanapali
Pkwy. (off Honoapiilani Hwy./
Hwy.30), in the Kaanapali Resort.*

kids Kamaole III Beach Park.
You can see why local residents love
this beach: Not only does it have
wide pockets of golden sand, it's the
only one with a playground for children and a grassy lawn. For snorkeling, look towards the rocky fingers

extending out in the north and
south shores, they are fish magnets.
*South Kihei Rd., across from
Keonekai Rd., Kihei.*

★★★ **Kapalua Beach.** I love
everything about this beach, located
next to the Kapalua Resort. The
water is so clear that you can not
only see where the gold sands turn
to green and then deep blue, but you
can stand on the beach and spot colorful tropical fish. Lava-rock promontories protect the water from strong
winds and currents, making it calm
for snorkeling, and jutting points at
either end of the beach attract lots of
fish. *Off Lower Honoapiilani Rd., next
door to the Napili Kai Beach Resort.*

Makena Landing. This bay is
popular with local residents on
weekends, but go on a weekday and
you could have it all to yourself. My
favorite snorkel tour is to follow the

Snorkeling in Kihei.

The Great Outdoors

Snorkeling with butterfly fish.

rocky shoreline looking for fish. *Along Makena Alanui, look for the shoreline access sign near the Makena Prince Hotel, turn right, and head down to the shore on Makena Rd.*

★★ **Molokini.** Like a crescent moon fallen from the sky, the crater of Molokini sits almost midway between Maui and the uninhabited island of Kahoolawe. On its concave side Molokini serves as a natural sanctuary for tropical fish and snorkelers, who arrive daily in a fleet of dive boats to this marine-life preserve. Note that in high season, Molokini can be crowded. See "Sail-snorkel Trips" on p 103 for information on getting to Molokini.

Where to Get Snorkel Gear

Snorkel Bob's (www.snorkelbob.com) has snorkel gear, boogie boards, and other ocean toys at four locations: 1217 Front St., Lahaina (☎ 808/661-4421); Napili Village, 5425-C Lower Honoapiilani Hwy., Napili (☎ 808/669-9603); in North Kihei at Azeka Place II, 1279 S. Kihei Rd. #310 (☎ 808/875-6188); and in South Kihei/Wailea at the Kamaole Beach Center, 2411 S. Kihei Rd., Kihei (☎ 808/879-7449). All locations are open daily from 8am to 5pm. If you're island-hopping, you can rent from a Snorkel Bob's location on one island and return it at a branch on another.

If you can't find a Snorkel Bob's close to you, my second pick is **Boss Frog's Dive and Surf Shops** (www.maui-vacation.net), with six stores: Napili Plaza, next to Subway (☎ 808/669-4949); Kahana Manor Shops, next to Dollies Pizza (☎ 808/669-6700); Kaanapali, 3636 L. Honoapiilani Rd. (☎ 808/665-1200); Lahaina, 150 Lahainaluna Rd. (☎ 808/661-3333); North Kihei, 1215 Kihei Rd. next to Long's Drugs Shopping Center (☎ 808/891-0077); and South Kihei, 2395 S. Kihei Rd., behind Pizza Hut at the Dolphin Plaza (☎ 808/875-4477).

Sail-snorkel Trips

★★★ **Trilogy** Trilogy tops the list of my favorite snorkel-sail trips. Hop aboard one of the fleet of custom-built catamarans for a half-day trip to Molokini. Trips leave from Maalaea Harbor and include breakfast and a barbecue lunch. ☎ 888/MAUI-800 or 808/TRILOGY. www.sailtrilogy.com. and costs $110 for adults, half-price for kids ages 3 to 12.

★★ **Maui Classic Charters** Morning and afternoon snorkel-sail cruises to Molokini on a 55-foot, glass-bottom catamaran, cost $84 adults ($49 children 3–12 years) for the morning sail and $40 adults ($30 children) in the afternoon. *Four Winds* trips include a continental breakfast; a barbecue lunch; complimentary beer, wine, and soda; complimentary snorkeling gear and instruction; and sportfishing along the way. Those looking for speed should book a trip on the fast, state-of-the-art catamaran, *Maui Magic*. The company offers a 5-hour snorkel journey to both Molokini and La Pérouse for $99 for adults and $79 for children ages 5 to 12, including a continental breakfast; barbecue lunch; beer, wine, and soda; snorkel gear; and instruction. During whale season (Dec 22–Apr 22), the *Four Winds* has a 3½-hour whale-watching trip for $42 adults and $30 children ages 3 to 12. *Maalaea Harbor, slip 55 and slip 80.* ☎ 800/736-5740 or 808/879-8188. www.mauicharters.com.

Pacific Whale Foundation This foundation supports its whale research by offering whale-watching cruises and snorkel tours, some to Molokini, on either their 65-foot power catamaran, or a 50-foot sailing catamaran, or another boat from their fleet. Choose from 15 daily trips, offered December through May, out of both Lahaina and Maalaea harbors. *101 N. Kihei Rd., Kihei.* ☎ 800/942-5311 or 808/879-8811. www.pacificwhale.org. Snorkeling cruises from $30.

Pride of Maui For a high-speed, action-packed snorkel-sail experience, consider the *Pride of Maui*. These 5½-hour snorkel cruises take in not only Molokini, but also Turtle Bay and Makena for more snorkeling; the cost is $86 for ages 13 and up and $53 for children ages 3 to 12. Continental breakfast, barbecue lunch, gear, and instruction are included. They also have an afternoon Molokini cruise ($35 for ages 13 and up and $27 for children ages 3–12, plus an optional lunch for an additional $5). *Maalaea Harbor.* ☎ 877/TO-PRIDE or 808/875-0955. www.prideofmaui.com.

Olowalu. Great snorkeling around MM14, where a turtle-cleaning station is about 150 to 225 feet (45m–67.5m) out from shore. Turtles line up here to have cleaner wrasses pick off small parasites. *MM14, Honoapiilani Hwy. 5 miles (8km) S of Lahaina.*

Ulua Beach. Snorkel here in the morning when the waters are calm and before local winds kick up around noon. *Look for the blue shoreline access sign, on Wailea Alanui Dr., Wailea.*

Adventures in the Ocean

0   5 mi

0   5 km

Honokohau Bay

Nakalele Point

Lipoa Point

Honolua Bay 4

Kapalua 5 Honokahua

Honokohau

Kahakuloa Head

PACIFIC OCEAN

Napili Bay

Kapalua Beach

Kahana

Honokowai

Kahakuloa

Hakuhee Point

WEST MAUI FOREST RESERVE

Waihee Point

Kaanapali

WEST MAUI MOUNTAINS

Hookipa Beach Park

Kahului Bay

Kanaha Beach Park 2

1

Kaanapali Beach

Lahaina 6

Puu Kukui

Waihee

3

Paia

Waikapu

Wailuku

Kahului

Kahului Airport

IAO VALLEY STATE PARK

WEST MAUI

Waikapu

Puunene

Honoapiilani Hwy.

Olowalu

Auau Channel

Maui Ocean Center

Maalaea 7

Kuihelani Hwy.

Mokulele Hwy.

Papawai Point

Maalaea Bay

Kihei

8

9

10

Piilani Hwy.

Kihei Rd.

11

12

SOUTH MAUI

PACIFIC OCEAN

Wailea Beach

Wailea

Mokapu & Ulua Beaches

13

Maluaka (Makena) Beach

Makena

Oneloa Beach (Big Beach)

Puu Olai

14

Molkini

Kanahena

Nukuele Point

Keoneoio

La Perouse Bay

Ulupalakua

Tedeschi Winery

15

KAHOOLAWE

Cape Hanamanioa

Alalakeiki Channel

Bodysurfing
Baldwin Beach 2
Mokuleia Beach 4
Kamaole III 12
Kapalua 5
Oneloa (Big Beach) 15
Ulua 13

Ocean Kayaking
Kihei Coast 9

Ocean Rafting 6

Sailing
Trilogy 6

Scuba Diving
Molokini 14

Sport Fishing
Lahaina 6
Maalaea 7

Surfing 2

Windsurfing
Hookipa Beach 1
Kanaha 3
Kihei 9
Maui Sunset 11
Ohukai Park 10

To really appreciate Maui, you need to get off the land and into the sea. Trade winds off the Lahaina Coast and the strong wind that rips through Maui's isthmus make sailing around the island exciting. Or you can go head-to-head with a 1,000-pound (453.6k) marlin in a big game fishing battle; slowly glide over the water in a kayak; hover high above it in a parasail; or get into the water and scuba dive, bodysurf, boardsurf, or windsurf.

Bodysurfing. Riding the waves without a board, becoming one with the rolling water is a way of life in Hawaii. Some bodysurfers just rely on their hands to ride the waves; others use hand boards or a boogie board or body board. Both body-surfing and body boarding require a pair of open-heeled swim fins to help propel you through the water. The best bodysurfing beaches are: **Baldwin Beach,** just outside of Paia, which has great waves nearly year-round; and in winter, **Mokuleia Beach,** known locally as Slaughter-house (for the cattle slaughterhouse that once stood here, not because of the waves—although they are definitely for expert bodysurfers only). Storms from the south bring fair bodysurfing conditions and great boogie boarding to the lee side of Maui: **Oneloa (Big Beach)** in Makena, **Ulua** and **Kamaole III** in Kihei, and **Kapalua** beaches are all good choices.

Ocean Kayaking. Gliding silently over the water, propelled by a paddle, seeing Maui from the sea the way the early Hawaiians did— that's what ocean kayaking is all about. One of Maui's best kayak routes is along the **Kihei Coast,** where there's easy access to calm water. Go out in the early mornings; the wind comes up around 11am, making seas choppy and paddling difficult.

Ocean Rafting. If you're semi-adventurous and looking for a more intimate experience with the sea, try ocean rafting. The inflatable rafts hold 6 to 24 passengers. Tours usually include snorkeling and coastal cruising. One of the best (and most reasonable) outfitters is **Hawaiian Ocean Raft;** their 5-hour tour includes three stops for snorkeling and stops to search for dolphins, plus continental breakfast and mid-morning snacks. *Lahaina Harbor,* ☎ *888/677-RAFT or 808/667-2191; www.hawaiioceanrafting.com. From $74 for adults and $53 for children ages 5–12.*

Craft along the Kihei Coast.

You might encounter a white tip reef shark like this one while diving.

Parasailing. Soar high above the crowds (at around 400 ft/122m.) for a bird's-eye view of Maui. This ocean adventure sport, which is something of a cross between skydiving and water-skiing, involves sailing through the air, suspended under a large parachute attached by a towline to a speedboat. Keep in mind, though, that parasailing tours don't run during whale season, which is roughly December through May. Book my favorite, the early-bird special (when the light is fantastic and the price is right) at 8am with **UFO Parasail,** which picks you up at Kaanapali Beach. (☎ *800/FLY-4-UFO or 808/661-7-UFO; www.ufoparasail.net). Early bird special is just $51 for 400 feet or $61 for 800 feet.*

Sailing. ★★★ **Trilogy** offers my favorite snorkel-sail trips. See the box on p 103 for more information.

Scuba Diving. You can see a great variety of tropical marine life—more than 100 endemic species found nowhere else on the planet—explore sea caves, and swim with sea turtles and monk seals in the clear tropical waters off the island. Trade winds often rough up the seas in the afternoon, so most operators schedule early-morning dives that end at noon. **Molokini** (see p 102), a marine-life park, is one of Hawaii's top dive spots. This crescent-shaped crater has three tiers of diving: a 35-foot plateau inside the crater basin (used by beginning divers and snorkelers), a wall sloping to 70 feet just beyond the inside plateau, and a sheer wall on the outside and backside of the crater that plunges 350 feet. This underwater park is very popular thanks to calm, clear, protected waters and an abundance of marine

Kayak Tours

My favorite kayak-tour operator is Makena Kayak Tours. Professional guide Dino Ventura leads a 2½-hour trip from Makena Landing and loves taking first-timers over the secluded coral reefs and into remote coves. His wonderful tour will be a highlight of your vacation. ☎ *877/879-8426 or 808/879-8426; www.makenakayaks.com. Cost: $55, including refreshments and snorkel and kayak equipment.*

In Hana, **Hana-Maui Sea Sports** runs 2-hour tours of Hana's coastline on wide, stable "no roll" kayaks, with snorkeling. ☎ *808/248-7711; www.hana-maui-seasports.com. Cost: $89 per person.*

Whale Watching

Every winter, pods of Pacific humpback whales make the 3,000-mile (4,830km) swim from the chilly waters of Alaska to bask in Maui's summery shallows. The whale-watching season usually begins in December or January and lasts until April or May. Bring binoculars to one of the following spots: **McGregor Point,** on the way to Lahaina, scenic lookout at MM 9; **Olowalu Reef,** along the straight part of Honoapiilani Hwy., between McGregor Point and Olowalu; ★★ **Puu Olai,** which is a tough climb, but the island's best spot for offshore whale-watching; or **Wailea Marriott Resort** (3700 Wailea Alanui Dr., Wailea), on the Wailea coastal walk, with a telescope installed for whale watching.

If you want to get a closer look, try the cruises offered by the nonprofit **Pacific Whale Foundation,** 101 N. Kihei Rd., Kihei (☎ 800/942-5311 or 808/879-8811; www.pacificwhale.org). Rates for a 2-hour cruise start at $20 for adults, $15 for children. Cruises are offered from December through May, out of both Lahaina and Maalaea harbors.

life, from manta rays to clouds of yellow butterfly fish. Most operators offer no-experience-necessary dives, ranging from $100 for one tank to $150 for two tanks. Maui's two best scuba operators are: **Ed Robinson's Diving Adventures** (☎ 800/635-1273; www.mauis cuba.com), charging $120 for two-tank dives ($135 with equipment); and **Mike Severns Diving** (☎ 808/879-6596; www.mike severnsdiving.com), where two-tank dives are $125 and $140 with rental equipment.

Sport Fishing. Marlin (as big as 1,200 lb./544.3k), tuna, ono, and mahimahi swim in Maui's coastal and channel waters. No license is required; just book a sport-fishing vessel out of **Lahaina** or **Maalaea** harbors. Most charter boats that troll for big-game fish carry a maximum of six passengers. You can walk the docks, inspecting boats and talking to captains and crews, or book through **Sportfish Hawaii**

(☎ 877/388-1376 or 808/396-2607; www.sportfishhawaii.com). Prices vary widely according to the boat, the crowd, and the captain. A shared boat for a half day of fishing starts at $100; a shared full day of fishing

Watching windsurfers is almost as much fun as trying the sport yourself.

The Great Outdoors

starts at around $250. A half-day exclusive (you get the entire boat) starts at $600; a full-day exclusive starts at $900. Many boat captains tag and release marlin or keep the fish for themselves (sorry, that's Hawaii style). If you want to eat your mahimahi for dinner or have your marlin mounted, tell the captain before you go.

Surfing. The ancient Hawaiian sport of *hee nalu* (wave sliding) is probably the sport most people picture when they think of the islands. If you'd like to give it a shot, call Tide and Kiva Rivers, two local boys (actually twins), who have been surfing since they could walk, and the best surf instructors I have seen. The lessons are 2-hours long and include equipment and instruction. Tide, who has been surfing for 25 years, says they decide where the lesson will take place based on their client's ability and where the surf is on that day. He says he has beginners standing up in their first lesson. *Rivers to the Sea.* ☎ *808/280-8795 or 808/280-6236; www.riverstothesea.com. Rates $75 group instruction.*

A playful whale.

Windsurfing. Maui has Hawaii's best windsurfing beaches. In winter, windsurfers from around the world flock to the town of Paia to ride the waves. **Hookipa Beach,** known all over the globe for its brisk winds and excellent waves, is the site of several world-championship contests. **Kanaha,** west of Kahului Airport, also has dependable winds. When the winds turn northerly, **Kihei** is the spot to be. The northern end of Kihei is best: **Ohukai Park,** the first beach as you enter South Kihei Rd. from the northern end, has not only good winds but parking, a long strip of grass to assemble your gear, and good access to the water. Experienced windsurfers can be found in front of the **Maui Sunset** condo, 1032 S. Kihei Rd., near Waipuilani St. (a block north of McDonald's), which has great windsurfing conditions but a very shallow reef (not good for beginners). For lessons contact **Hawaiian Island Surf and Sport,** *415 Dairy Rd., Kahului (☎ 800/231-6958 or 808/871-4981; www.hawaiianisland.com). From $79.* ●

Lodging Best Bets

Most Romantic
★ Hamoa Bay Bungalow $$ *Hana Hwy., Hana (p 115)*

Most Historic
★★ Old Wailuku Inn at Ulupono $$ *2199 Kahookele St., Wailuku (p 117)*

Most Luxurious Hotel
★★★ The Fairmont Kea Lani Maui $$$$$ *4100 Wailea Alanui Dr., Wailea (p 114)*

Most Luxurious Condo
★★ Kaanapali Alii $$$$ *50 Nohea Kai Dr., Kaanapali (p 116)*

Best Moderate Hotel
★ Lahaina Inn $$ *127 Lahainaluna Rd., Lahaina (p 116)*

Best Budget Hotel
★ Nona Lani Cottages $ *455 S. Kihei Rd., Kihei (p 117)*

Best for Kids
★★★ Four Seasons Resort Maui at Wailea $$$$$ *3900 Wailea Alanui Dr., Wailea (p 114)*

Best Value
★★ Pineapple Inn Maui $ *3170 Akala Dr., Kihei (p 117)*

Most Charming B&B
★★ Wild Ginger Falls $ *355 Kaluanui Rd., Makawao (p 118)*

Best View
★★ Napili Kai Beach Resort $$$ *5900 Honoapiilani Rd., Napali (p 117)*

Best Club-Level Amenities
★★★ Ritz-Carlton Kapalua $$$$ *1 Ritz-Carlton Dr., Kapalua (p 117)*

Best Service
★★★ Four Seasons Resort Maui at Wailea $$$$$ *3900 Wailea Alanui Dr., Wailea (p 114)*

Best Spa
★★★ Grand Wailea Resort Hotel & Spa $$$$$ *3850 Wailea Alanui Dr., Wailea (p 115)*

Most Hawaiian Resort
★★★ Hotel Hana-Maui $$$$$ *Hana Hwy., Hana (p 115)* and ★ Kaanapali Beach Hotel $$ *2525 Kaanapali Pkwy., Kaanapali (p 116)*

Most Secluded
★★ Olinda Country Cottages & Inn $$ *2660 Olinda Rd., Makawao (p 117)*

Best Fantasy Resort
★★ Hyatt Regency Maui Resort and Spa $$$$ *200 Nohea Kai Dr., Kaanapali (p 116)*

Best Off the Beaten Path
★★ The Inn at Mama's Fish House $$ *799 Poho Pl., Kuau (p 116)*

Most Eco-Friendly
★ Westin Maui $$$$$ *2365 Kaanapali Pkwy., Kaanapali (p 118)*

Most Serene Location
★★ Hana Oceanfront $$ *Haneoo Rd., Hana (p 115)*

Best Family Condo
★ Maui Eldorado Resort $$$ *2661 Kekaa Dr., Kaanapali (p 116)*

A room at the Kaanapali Beach Hotel.

Maui & Kapalua Lodging

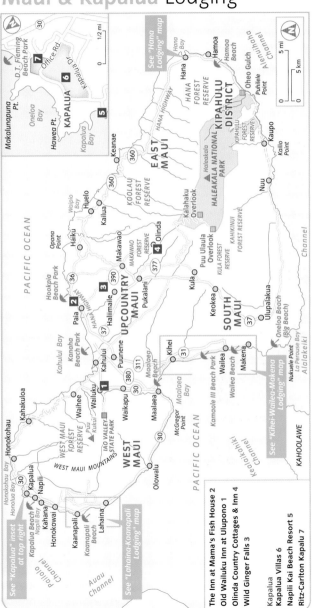

The Inn at Mama's Fish House 2
Old Wailuku Inn at Ulupono 1
Olinda Country Cottages & Inn 4
Wild Ginger Falls 3

Kapalua
Kapalua Villas 6
Napili Kai Beach Resort 5
Ritz-Carlton Kapalu 7

Lahaina & Kaanapali Lodging

Best Western Pioneer Inn 10
Hyatt Regency Maui Resort and Spa 7
Kaanapali Alii 6
Kaanapali Beach Hotel 3
Lahaina Inn 8
Maui Eldorado Resort 1
The Plantation Inn 9
Sheraton Maui 2
Westin Maui 5
The Whaler on Kaanapali Beach 5

Kihei/Wailea/Makena Lodging

The Fairmont Kea Lani Maui 6
Four Seasons Resort Maui at Wailea 5
Grand Wailea Resort Hotel & Spa 4
Maui Prince Hotel 7
Nona Lani Cottages 1
Pineapple Inn Maui 2
Wailea Marriott Resort & Spa 3

Hana Lodging

Hamoa Bay Bungalow 3
Hana Oceanfront 4
Heavenly Hana Inn 1
Hotel Hana-Maui 2

Maui Hotels A to Z

kids Best Western Pioneer Inn
LAHAINA   This turn-of-the-19th-century, two-story, plantation-style hotel overlooking the Lahaina harbor has been remodeled with vintage bathrooms. *658 Wharf St. (in front of Lahaina Pier).* ☎ *800/457-5457 or 808/661-3636; www.pioneerinnmaui. com. 34 units. Doubles $115–$180. Extra person $15 (12 or older). AE, DC, DISC, MC, V. Map p 112.*

★★★ The Fairmont Kea Lani Maui WAILEA   You get your money's worth at this luxurious resort: an entire suite—plus a kitchenette, entertainment center, sofa bed, spacious bedroom, and large lanai. *4100 Wailea Alanui Dr.* ☎ *800/659-4100 or 808/875-4100;*

www.fairmont.com/kealani. 450 units. Doubles $395–$895. AE, DC, DISC, MC, V. Map p 113.

★★★ kids Four Seasons Resort Maui at Wailea WAILEA
The Four Seasons has attentive but not cloying service, and it's the most kid-friendly hotel on Maui, with cookies and milk on arrival, children's menus, and complimentary baby gear (cribs to strollers). You can even pre-purchase necessities like diapers and baby food; the hotel will have them waiting for you when you arrive. *3900 Wailea Alanui Dr.* ☎ *800/334-MAUI or 808/874-8000; www.fourseasons.com/maui. 380 units. Doubles $395–$790. AE, DC, MC, V. Map p 113.*

The Four Seasons Resort.

★★★ Grand Wailea Resort Hotel & Spa
WAILEA   Hawaii's largest and most elaborate spa, with every kind of body treatment you can imagine, plus the use of the numerous baths, hot tubs, mineral pools, saunas, and steam rooms. *3850 Wailea Alanui Dr.* ☎ *800/888-6100 or 808/875-1234; www.grand wailea.com. 780 units. Doubles $495–$905 double. AE, DC, DISC, MC, V. Map p 113.*

★ Hamoa Bay Bungalow
HANA Romance blooms in a 600-square-foot (55.75m sq.) Balinese-style tree-top studio with a hot tub and a beckoning bamboo bed. Plus, you're close to Hamoa Beach. *P.O. Box 773.* ☎ *808/248-7853; www.hamoabay. com. 2 units. Doubles $195. MC, V. Map p 114.*

★★ Hana Oceanfront
HANA Serenity reigns at these two comfy, plantation-style cottages (polished bamboo flooring and fully appointed gourmet kitchen), just across the street from Hamoa Bay. *P.O. Box 843.* ☎ *808/248-7558; www.hanaocean frontcottages.com. 2 units. Doubles $225–$250. MC, V. Map p 114.*

★★ Heavenly Hana Inn
HANA In this Japanese-style inn each suite has a sitting room, polished hardwood floors, a separate bedroom with a raised platform bed, and a black-marble soaking tub. *P.O. Box 790.* ☎ *808/248-8442; www.heavenlyhanainn.com. 3 units. Doubles $190–$260. AE, DISC, MC, V. Map p 114.*

★★★ kids Hotel Hana-Maui
HANA The atmosphere and the culture of old Hawaii is set within 21st-century accommodations on 66 rolling seaside acres. Throw in an excellent spa, and one of Hana's best beaches, and you'll never want to leave. *P.O. Box 9.* ☎ *800/321-HANA or 808/248-8211; www.hotel hanamaui.com. 66 units. Doubles $425–$995. AE, DC, DISC, MC, V. Map p 114.*

The pool at the Grand Wailea Resort.

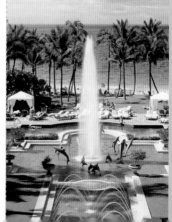

★★ **kids** **Hyatt Regency Maui Resort & Spa** KAANAPALI This fantasy resort has a ½-acre (0.2 hectare) outdoor pool with a 150-foot (45m) lava tube slide, a cocktail bar under the falls, nine waterfalls, exotic birds in the lobby, and an eclectic Asian and Pacific art collection. *200 Nohea Kai Dr.* ☎ *800/233-1234 or 808/661-1234; www.maui.hyatt.com. 806 units. Doubles $365–$765. AE, DC, DISC, MC, V. Map p 112.*

★★ **The Inn at Mama's Fish House** PAIA Off the beaten path in a coconut grove on secluded Kuau Beach, these expertly decorated duplexes sit next door to Mama's Fish House (guests get a discount on meals). *799 Poho Place (off the Hana Hwy. in Kuau).* ☎ *800/860-HULA or 808/579-9764; www.mamasfish house.com. 6 units. Doubles $175–$475. AE, DISC, MC, V. Map p 111.*

★★ **kids** **Kaanapali Alii** KAANA-PALI These oceanfront condominium units sit on 8 landscaped acres (3.2 hectares) right on Kaanapali Beach and combine all the amenities of a luxury hotel with the convenience of a condominium. There's even a yoga class Mondays, Wednesdays, and Fridays on the lawn. *50 Nohea Kai Dr.* ☎ *800/642-6284 or 808/661-3330; www. kaanapali-alii.com. 264 units. Doubles $330–$685. AE, DC, DISC, MC, V. Map p 112.*

A room at the Hotel Hana-Maui.

★ **kids** **Kaanapali Beach Hotel** KAANAPALI Old Hawaii values and customs reign here; you'll see them in everything from the nightly Hawaiian hula and music to the extensive Hawaiiana program (learn to cut pineapple, weave lauhala, even dance the *real* hula). *2525 Kaanapali Pkwy.* ☎ *800/262-8450 or 808/661-0011; www.kbhmaui.com. 430 units. Doubles $185–$325. AE, DC, DISC, MC, V. Map p 112.*

★★ **kids** **Kapalua Villas** KAPALUA The palatial condo units dotting the oceanfront cliffs and fairways of this idyllic coast are a (relative) bargain, especially for big families. *500 Office Rd.* ☎ *800/545-0018 or 808/669-8088; www.kapalua villas.com. Doubles $259–$279 1-bedroom; $359–$379 2-bedrooms; $479–$499 3-bedrooms. AE, DC, DISC, MC, V. Map p 111.*

★ **Lahaina Inn** LAHAINA These Victorian antique–stuffed rooms are a rare bargain on Maui, with an excellent restaurant and bar downstairs (David Paul's Lahaina Grill, p. 126). However, rooms are on the small side. *127 Lahainaluna Rd. (near Front St.).* ☎ *800/669-3444 or 808/661-0577; www.lahainainn.com. 12 units. Doubles $130–$150. AE, MC, V. Map p 112.*

★ **kids** **Maui Eldorado Resort** KAANAPALI These are the best condos for families: spacious units, grassy play areas outside, safe swimming, and a beachfront beach with cabanas and barbecue area. *2661 Kekaa Dr.* ☎ *800/688-7444 or 808/ 661-0021; www.outrigger.com. 204 units. Doubles $219–$259 studio; $269–$309 1-bedroom; $369–$479 2-bedrooms. AE, DC, DISC, MC, V. Map p 112.*

★★ **Maui Prince Hotel** MAKENA Tranquility and a golden-sand beach are what you'll find at this end-of-the-road resort where every clutter-free

Kapalua Villas.

room has an ocean view. *5400 Makena Alanui.* ☎ *800/321-6284 or 808/874-1111; www.mauiprincehotel.com. 310 units. Doubles $355–$525. AE, DC, MC, V. Map p 113.*

★★ kids **Napili Kai Beach Resort** NAPILI   Ocean views of Molokai and Lanai, Hawaii-style architecture, a secluded gold-sand beach, and a choice of hotel rooms or condos make this resort very popular. *5900 Honoapiilani Rd. (at the extreme north end of Napili, next to Kapalua Resort).* ☎ *800/367-5030 or 808/669-6271; www.napilikai. com. 162 units. Doubles $210–$250 hotel room; $265–$310 studio; $400 1-bedroom; $560–$575 2-bedrooms. AE, DISC, MC, V. Map p 111.*

★ **Nona Lani Cottages** KIHEI   These self-contained cottages tucked among palm, fruit, and sweet-smelling flower trees and across the street from a white-sand beach, are the best deal on Maui. *455 S. Kihei Rd. (just south of Hwy. 31), P.O. Box 655.* ☎ *800/733-2688 or 808/879-2497; www.nonalanicottages.com. 11 units. Double $90–$120. No credit cards. Map p 113.*

★★ **Old Wailuku Inn at Ulupono** WAILUKU   This lovingly restored 1924 former plantation manager's home offers a genuine old Hawaii experience, plus a gourmet breakfast. *2199 Kahookele St. (at High St., across from the Wailuku School).* ☎ *800/305-4899 or 808/244-5897; www.mauiinn.com. 10 units. Double $140–$190. MC, V. Map p 111.*

★★ **Olinda Country Cottages & Inn** MAKAWAO   Hidden on the slopes of Haleakala on an 8½-acre (3.4 hectare) farm dotted with protea plants and surrounded by 35,000 acres (14,000 hectares) of ranch lands, these cottages are perfect for those looking for a secluded vacation. *2660 Olinda Rd. (near the top of Olinda Rd., a 15-min. drive from Makawao).* ☎ *800/932-3435 or 808/572-1453; www.mauibnbcottages. com. 5 units. Double $140; cottage $195–$245. No credit cards. Map p 117.*

★★ **Pineapple Inn Maui** KIHEI   This charming inn offers impeccably decorated, soundproof rooms, a giant saltwater pool and Jacuzzi overlooking the ocean, and wallet-pleasing prices. *3170 Akala Dr.* ☎ *877/212-MAUI (6284) or 808/298-4403; www.pineappleinnmaui.com. Double $109–$139; cottage $185. No credit cards. Map p 113.*

★★ **The Plantation Inn** LAHAINA   This romantic, Victorian-style inn features period furniture and four-poster canopy beds. It's next door to one of Lahaina's best French restaurants (guests get a discount), Gerard's, see p 126. *174 Lahainaluna Rd. (between Wainee and Luakini sts., 1 block from Hwy. 30).* ☎ *800/433-6815 or 808/667-9225; www.theplantationinn.com. 19 units. Double $160–$225. AE, DC, DISC, MC, V. Map p 112.*

★★★ kids **Ritz-Carlton Kapalua** KAPALUA   If you can afford it, stay on the Club Floor, which offers the best amenities in the state, including French-roast coffee in the morning, a buffet at lunch, cookies in the afternoon, and pupus and drinks at sunset. *1 Ritz-Carlton Dr.* ☎ *800/262-8440 or 808/669-6200; www.ritz carlton.com. 548 units. Double $365–$675; Club Floor from $900. AE, DC, DISC, MC, V. Map p 111.*

★★ **kids** **Sheraton Maui** KAANAPALI   The family suites are great for those traveling with kids: three beds, a sitting room with full-size couch, and two TVs (both equipped with Nintendo); plus fun activities ranging from Hawaiian games to visits to nearby attractions. *2605 Kaanapali Pkwy.* ☎ *888/488-3535 or 808/661-0031; www.sheraton-maui.com. 510 units. Double $405–$695. AE, DC, DISC, MC, V. Map p 112.*

★★ **Wailea Marriott Resort & Spa** WAILEA   This classic open-air, 1970s-style hotel in a tropical garden by the sea gives you a sense of what Maui was like before the big resort boom. *3700 Wailea Alanui Dr.* ☎ *800/367-2960 or 808/879-1922; www.marriott hawaii.com. 545 units. Doubles $475–$800. AE, DC, DISC, MC, V. Map p 113.*

Napili Kai Beach Resort.

★ **kids** **Westin Maui** KAANAPALI   This resort emphasizes a healthy environment, and smoking is no longer allowed in guest rooms (it is allowed in some public areas). Kids will love the aquatic playground. *2365 Kaanapali Pkwy.* ☎ *888/625-4949 or 808/667-2525; Fax 808/661-5764; www.westinmaui.com. 758 units. Double $440–$710. AE, DC, DISC, MC, V. Map p 112.*

★★ **The Whaler on Kaanapali Beach** KAANAPALI   In the heart of Kaanapali, right on the world-famous beach, lies this condo oasis of elegance, privacy, and luxury. *2481 Kaanapali Pkwy. (next to Whalers Village).* ☎ *877/997-6667 or 808/661-4861; www.resortquesthawaii.com. 360 units. Double $235–$310; $280–$500 1-bedroom; $380–$730 2-bedroom. AE, DC, DISC, MC, V. Map p 112.*

★★ **Wild Ginger Falls** MAKAWAO   Perfect for honeymooners and lovers: this cozy, romantic, intimate cottage, hidden in Miliko Gulch, overlooks a stream with a waterfall, bamboo, sweet-smelling ginger, and banana trees. *355 Kaluanui Rd.* ☎ *808/573-1173; www.wildginger falls.com. 1 unit. Double $135–$145. No credit cards. Map p 111.* ●

Dining Best Bets

Best on the Beach
★ **kids** Hula Grill $$$ *Whaler's Village, Kaanapali (p 127)*

Best Breakfast
★ **kids** Charlie's Restaurant $$ *142 Hana Hwy., Paia (p 125)* and ★★ Longhi's $$$$ *Shops at Wailea (p 128)*

Best Burger
kids Cheeseburger in Paradise $ *811 Front St., Lahaina (p 126)*

Best Budget Deli
★ **kids** CJ's Deli and Diner $ *Kaanapali Fairway Shops (p 125)*

Best Crepes
Café des Amis $$ *42 Baldwin, Paia (p 125)*

Best for Families
★ **kids** Stella Blues $$ *Azeka II Shopping Center, Kihei (p 130)*

Best French
★★★ Gerard's $$$$ *174 Lahainaluna Rd., Lahaina (p 126)*

Freshest Fish
★★★ Pineapple Grill Kapalua $$$ *200 Kapalua Dr (p 129)*

Best Italian
★★ Vino Italian Tapas & Wine Bar $$$$ *Kapalua Village Course Golf Club House (p 130)*

Best Luau
★★★ **kids** Old Lahaina Luau $$$$$ *1251 Front St., Lahaina (p 125)*

Best Fast Mexican
kids Maui Tacos $ *Napili Lahaina Kihei Kahului (p 128)*

Best Pasta
★ Caffé Ciao $$$ *Fairmont Kea Lani Hotel (p 125)*

Best People Watching
★ Milagros Food Company $$ *Hana Hwy., Paia (p 129)*

Best Pizza
kids Shaka Sandwich & Pizza $$ *1770 S. Kihei Rd., Kihei (p 130)*

Most Romantic
★★ Lahaina Store Grille and Oyster Bar $$$ *744 Front St., Lahaina (p 128)*

Best Splurge
★★★ Mama's Fish House $$$$ *799 Poho Pl., Kuau (p 128)*

Best Sushi
★★ Sansei Seafood Restaurant and Sushi Bar $$$ *Office Rd., Kapalua (p 130)*

Most Trendy
★★ **kids** David Paul's Lahaina Grill $$$$ *127 Lahainaluna Rd., Lahaina (p 126)*

Best Meal Under $10
Joy's Place $ *1993 S. Kihei Rd., Kihei (p 127)*

Best View
★ **kids** Kula Lodge $$$ *Haleakala Hwy., Kula (p 128)*

Enjoying a sunset meal at the Pineapple Grill.

Maui & Paia **Dining**

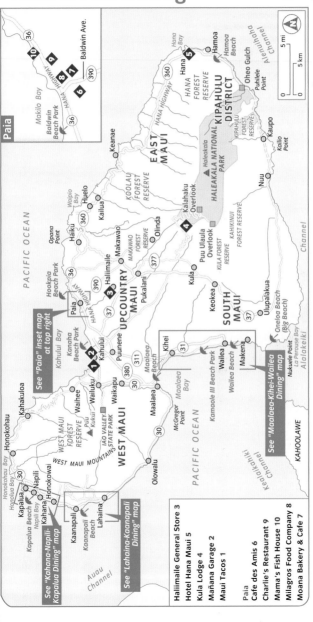

Haliimaile General Store 3
Hotel Hana Maui 5
Kula Lodge 4
Mañana Garage 2
Maui Tacos 1

Paia
Cafe des Amis 6
Charlie's Restaurant 9
Mama's Fish House 10
Milagros Food Company 8
Moana Bakery & Cafe 7

Lahaina & Kaanapali Dining

CJ's Deli and Diner 1
Cheeseburger in Paradise 5
Chez Paul 11
David Paul's Lahaina Grill 6
The Feast at Lele 10
Gerard's 7
Hula Grill 2
Lahaina Coolers 9
Lahaina Store Grille and Oyster Bar 8
Maui Tacos 4
Old Lahaina Luau 3

Kekaa Dr.

LK & P Sugar Cane Train

Kaanapali North
Golf Course

Whalers Village

Honoapiilani Hwy.

KAANAPALI

Kaanapali Parkway

Kaanapaii
Golf Courses
Club House

Nohea Kai Dr.

Kaanapali South
Golf Course

Hanakaoo
Beach Park

Wahikuli
Beach Park

Lahaina
Civic Center

Post
Office

Auau Channel

Lahaina
Cannery Mall

Kapunakea
St.

Mala Wharf

Honoapiilani Hwy.

Kahoma Stream

Lahainaluna
School
(1837)

Hilo
Hattie

Train Depot

Pioneer
Sugar Mill

Lahainaluna Rd.

Lahaina Center

Papalaua St.

LAHAINA

Front St.

Dickenson St.

Baldwin Home Museum

Wainee St.

Luakini St.

Prison St.

Lahaina
Small Boat Harbor

Banyan Tree

505 Front St.
(Shops & Restaurants)

Shaw St.

0   1/2 mi
0   0.5 km

MAUI

Kaanapali
Lahaina

Kahana, Napili & Kapalua **Dining**

0   1 mi
0   1 km

Mokuleia Bay

Plantation House

Plantation Course

D.T. Fleming Beach Park

Makalunapuna Pt.

Oneloa Bay

Hawea Pt.

KAPALUA

Kapalua Bay

Office Rd.

Bay Course

Kapalua Dr.

30

Village Course

Napili Bay

Lower Honoapiilani Rd.

NAPILI

Honoapiilani Highway

Napili Plaza

KAHANA

Hoohui Rd.

Akahele St.

Kapalua West-Maui Airport

Lower Honoapiilani Rd.

HONOKOWAI

30

Kapalua
Napili
Kahana

MAUI

Maui Tacos 4
Pineapple Grill Kapalua 3
Roy's Kahana Bar & Grill 5
Sansei Seafood Restaurant and Sushi Bar 2
Vino Italian Tapas & Wine Bar 1

Maalaea, Kihei & Wailea Dining

Caffé Ciao 9
Joe's Bar & Grill 7
Joy's Place 5
Longhi's 8
Maui Tacos 6
Peggy Sue's 3
The Place 1
Shaka Sandwich & Pizza 4
Stella Blues Cafe 2
The Waterfront at Maalaea 1

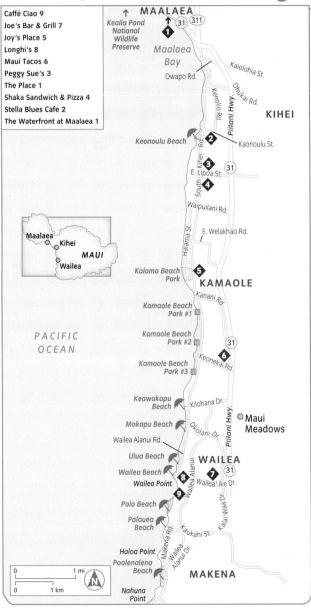

MAALAEA

Kealia Pond National Wildlife Preserve

Maalaea Bay

Kaiolohia St.

Owapo Rd.

Kenolio Rd.

Ohukai Rd.

Piilani Hwy.

KIHEI

Keonoulu Beach

Kaonoulu St.

South Kihei Rd.

E. Lipoa St.

Waipuilani Rd.

Halama St.

E. Welakhao Rd.

Kalama Beach Park

KAMAOLE

Kanani Rd.

Kamaole Beach Park #1

Kamaole Beach Park #2

Keonekai Rd.

PACIFIC OCEAN

Kamaole Beach Park #3

Keawakapu Beach

Kilohana Dr.

Maui Meadows

Mokapu Beach

Okolani Dr.

Wailea Alanui Rd.

Ulua Beach

WAILEA

Wailea Beach

Wailea 'Ike Dr.

Wailea Point

Wailea Alanui

Polo Beach

Kalai-Naa Dr.

Palauea Beach

Haloa Point

Makena Rd.

Wailea Alanui Dr.

Kaukahi St.

Poolenalena Beach

MAKENA

Nahuna Point

Maalaea
Kihei
MAUI
Wailea

0   1 mi
0   1 km
N

Maui Restaurants A to Z

★ kids CJ's Deli and Diner

KAANAPALI *AMERICAN/DELI* It's worth the drive to sample the comfort food at this hip, happening deli, with prices so low you won't believe you're still on Maui. *Kaanapali Fairway Shops, 2580 Keka'a Dr. (just off the Honoapiilani Hwy/Hwy. 30.).* ☎ *808/667-0968. Breakfast items $3–$9.50; lunch $7–$12. AE, MC, V. Breakfast, lunch & dinner daily. Map p 122.*

★★ Cafe des Amis PAIA

CREPES/MEDITERRANEAN/INDIAN Crepes are the star here, just edging out the incredibly cheap authentic Indian curries. Finish with the best coffee in Paia. *42 Baldwin Ave.* ☎ *808/579-6323. Breakfast crepes $8–$9. Lunch crepes $7.25–$9. Dinner entrees $11–$15. MC, V. Breakfast, lunch & dinner daily. Map p 121.*

★ Caffé Ciao WAILEA *ITALIAN*

This charming trattoria not only has an elegant and reasonably priced outdoor restaurant, but also an

The Old Lahaina Luau is a feast for the eyes and the palate.

everything-thing-you-could-possibly-want-to-take-out deli. *Fairmont Kea Lani Hotel, 4100 Wailea Alanui.* ☎ *808/875-4100. Main courses $13–$20 lunch, $17–$36 dinner; pizzas $17–$19. AE, DC, DISC, MC, V. Lunch (seasonally), dinner daily. Map p 124.*

★ kids Charlie's Restaurant

PAIA *AMERICAN/MEXICAN* Offering one of the best breakfasts on Maui, this landmark is a mix of a 1960s

Old Lahaina Luau

Maui's best luau features terrific food and entertainment in a peerless, oceanfront setting. The luau begins at sunset and features Tahitian and Hawaiian entertainment, including ancient hula, hula from the missionary era, modern hula, and an intelligent narrative on the dance's rocky course of survival into modern times. The entertainment is riveting, even for jaded locals. The high-quality food, served from an open-air thatched structure, is as much Pacific Rim as authentically Hawaiian: imu-roasted Kalua pig, baked mahimahi in Maui-onion cream sauce, guava chicken, teriyaki sirloin steak, lomi salmon, poi, dried fish, poke, Hawaiian sweet potato, sautéed vegetables, seafood salad, and the ultimate treat, taro leaves with coconut milk. 1251 Front St., Lahaina (☎ 800/248-5828 or 808/667-1998. www.oldlahainaluau.com). The cost is $89 for adults, $59 for children 12 and under.

hippie hangout, a windsurfers' power-breakfast spot, and a honky-tonk bar that gets going after dark. *142 Hana Hwy.* ☎ *808/579-9453. Breakfast items around $3.75–$12; lunch items $7.95–$12; dinner main courses $10–$22. AE, DISC, MC, V. Breakfast, lunch & dinner daily. Map p 121.*

kids Cheeseburger in Paradise
LAHAINA *AMERICAN* Always crowded and noisy (with live music every night), this shrine to the American classic is a good value. It has great grinds and a killer ocean view. *811 Front St.* ☎ *808/661-4855. Burgers $7–$10. AE, DISC, MC, V. Breakfast, lunch & dinner daily. Map p 122.*

★★ Chez Paul OLOWALU *FRENCH* In the middle of nowhere, this classic French restaurant offers elegant food in a casual setting, pricey but worth every penny. *MM15, Honoapiilani Hwy.* ☎ *808/661-3843; www. chezpaul.net. Main courses $29–$39. DISC, MC, V. Dinner daily. Map p 122.*

★★ kids David Paul's Lahaina Grill LAHAINA *NEW AMERICAN* The chic flock to this hot spot for tequila shrimp with firecracker rice, Kona coffee–roasted rack of lamb, Maui onion–crusted seared ahi, and Kalua duck quesadilla. There's a special kids' menu. *127 Lahainaluna Rd.*

Seared ahi at David Paul's Lahaina Grill.

Haliimaile General Store.

☎ *808/667-5117; www.lahainagrill. com. Main courses $26–$62; $74 tasting menu. AE, DC, DISC, MC, V. Dinner daily 5:30–10pm. Map p 122.*

★★ The Feast at Lele LAHAINA *POLYNESIAN* Taking Luau cuisine to a new level, the owners of Old Lahaina Luau (p 125) provide the food and dances from Hawaii, Tonga, Tahiti, Cook, New Zealand, and Samoa in an outdoor setting with white-clothed, candlelit tables set on the sand and entrees from each island. *505 Front St.* ☎ *886/244-5353 or 808/667-5353; www.feastatlele.com. Set 5-course menu $105 for adults, $75 for children 2–12; gratuity not included. AE, MC, V. Dinner daily. Map p 122.*

★★★ Gerard's LAHAINA *FRENCH* Chef Gerard Reversade (a frequent winner of the *Wine Spectator* Award of Excellence) is at the helm of this creative French cuisine in an elegant Victorian home. *In the Plantation Inn, 174 Lahainaluna Rd.* ☎ *808/ 661-8939; www.gerardsmaui. com. Main courses $30–$50. AE, DC, DISC, MC, V. Dinner daily. Map p 122.*

★★★ kids Haliimaile General Store HALIIMAILE *AMERICAN* Chef Bev Gannon, 1 of the 12 original Hawaii Regional Cuisine chefs, heads up this foodie haven in the pineapple fields with her innovative spin on good ol' American cuisine, bringing Hawaiian and Texas flavors together. *Haliimaile Rd.* ☎ *808/572-2666; www.haliimailegeneral store.com. Lunch $10–$20; dinner $22–$39. AE, DC, DISC, MC, V. Lunch Mon–Fri, dinner daily. Map p 121.*

★★★ **Hotel Hana Maui** HANA *ECLECTIC* This ingredient-driven menu (fresh fish caught by local fishermen, produce grown by nearby farmers, and fruits in season) is served in the graceful setting of the open-aired, large window dining room. Not cheap, but worth it. *Hana Hwy.* ☎ *808/248-8211. Entrees $13–$18 breakfast, $10–$21 lunch, $31–$36 dinner; tasting menu $55 for 3 courses, $67 for 4 courses, $75 for Chef's Choice. AE, DISC, MC, V. Breakfast, lunch & dinner daily. Friday buffet $50 and Hawaiian show 6–8:30pm. Map p 121.*

★ **kids Hula Grill** KAANAPALI *HAWAII REGIONAL/SEAFOOD* Skip the main dining room and dig your toes in the sand at the Barefoot Bar on the beach, where you can chow down on burgers, fish, pizza, and salad. *Whalers Village, 2435 Kaanapali Pkwy.* ☎ *808/667-6636; www.hulagrill.com. Lunch and Barefoot Bar menus $8–$16; dinner main*

Roselani's coconut ice cream.

courses $18–$32. AE, DC, DISC, MC, V. Lunch, dinner daily. Map p 122.

★★ **Joe's Bar & Grill** WAILEA *AMERICAN GRILL* The 270-degree view of the golf course, tennis courts, ocean, and Haleakala is secondary to Chef Beverly Gannon's (see Haliimaile General Store, p 126) American home cooking, from meatloaf to roasted portabella mushrooms. *Wailea Tennis Club, 131 Wailea Ike Place.* ☎ *808/875-7767. Main courses $20–$32. AE, DC, DISC, MC, V. Dinner daily. Map p 124.*

Joy's Place KIHEI *HEALTHY DELI/ SANDWICHES* If you are in Kihei and are looking for a healthy, delicious lunch at a rock-bottom price, it's worth hunting around for this tiny hole in the wall with humongous

Maui's Best Ice Cream: Roselani

Aloha ice cream aficionados: For the culinary experience of your trip, try **Roselani Ice Cream,** Maui's only made-from-scratch, old-fashioned ice cream. There are more than 40 different flavors to try, ranging from traditional vanilla to haupia (made from coconut and macadamia nut), or the popular chocolate macadamia nut, or Kona mud pie, or mango and cream, or coconut pineapple, or my favorite, luau fudge pie. For a list of hotels, restaurants, parlors, and grocery stores carrying Roselani, either call ☎ 808/244-7951 or check online at www.roselani.com.

sandwiches, fresh salads, hot soups, and yummy desserts. *Island Surf Building, 1993 S. Kihei Rd. (entrance to the restaurant is on Auhana St.).* ☎ 808/879-9258. *All items under $10. No credit cards. Mon–Sat 10am–5pm. Map p 124.*

★★ kids **Kula Lodge** KULA HAWAII *REGIONAL/AMERICAN* Huge breakfasts and awe-inspiring views, this upcountry lodge is a must for visitors going up (or down) Haleakala. *Haleakala Hwy. (Hwy. 377).* ☎ 808/878-2517; www.kulalodge.com. *Breakfast $7.50–$16; lunch $11–$18; dinner main courses $14–$28. AE, DC, DISC, MC, V. Breakfast, lunch & dinner daily. Map p 121.*

★ kids **Lahaina Coolers** LAHAINA *AMERICAN/INTERNATIONAL* This ultracasual indoor/outdoor restaurant is a hangout for hungry surfers on a tight budget. *180 Dickensen St.* ☎ 808/661-7082; www.lahaina coolers.com. *Main courses $7.50–$11 lunch, $14–$25 dinner. AE, DC, DISC, MC, V. Breakfast, lunch & dinner daily. Map p 122.*

★★ **Lahaina Store Grille and Oyster Bar** LAHAINA *MAUI ISLAND CUISINE/OYSTER BAR* Get a reservation for sunset on the roof top of this historic 1916 building and be prepared to eat some of the best food on Maui. *Foodies* may want to request the table inside the exhibition kitchen, where Chef Klink shows off his culinary talents. *744 Front St.* ☎ 808/661-9090; www.lahainastore grille.com. *Lunch entrees $12–$16; dinner entrees $18–$32. MC, V. Main dining room, oyster bar & bar lunch, dinner daily; rooftop dinner daily 5–10pm. Map p 122.*

★★ **Longhi's** WAILEA *ITALIAN* The open-air room, black-and-white checkered floor, and yummy Italian cuisine (terrific breakfasts) make this an essential Wailea stop. *The Shops at Wailea, 3750 Wailea Alanui Dr.* ☎ 808/891-8883; www.longhi-maui. com. *Breakfast $8.50–$20; lunch $8.50–$30; dinner $28–$80. AE, DC, MC, V. Breakfast, lunch & dinner daily. Map p 124.*

★★★ **Mama's Fish House** KUAU *SEAFOOD* On the beach, this South Seas fantasy worthy of Gauguin serves the most expensive (but worth every penny) fresh fish on Maui. *799 Poho Place, just off the Hana Hwy.* ☎ 808/579-8488; www. mamasfishhouse.com. *Main courses $29–$36 lunch, $35–$55 dinner. AE, DC, DISC, MC, V. Lunch & dinner daily. Map p 121.*

★★ kids **Mañana Garage** KAHULUI *LATIN AMERICAN* An industrial motif that includes hubcap-like table bases, a vertical garage door as a divider for private parties, and gleaming chrome and cobalt walls hints at the brilliantly conceived and executed cuisine (from fried green tomatoes to barbecued ribs). *33 Lono Ave.* ☎ 808/873-0220. *Lunch main courses $7–$13; dinner main courses $16–$29. AE, DISC, MC, V. Lunch & dinner Mon–Sat. Dinner Sun. Map p 121.*

kids **Maui Tacos** NAPALI, LAHAINA, KIHEI, KAHULUI *MEXICAN* Hungry surfers, discerning diners, burrito buffs, and Hollywood glitterati flock to this fast, healthy, and cheap taco chain, where gourmet Mexican is served on paper plates. *In Napili Plaza, 5095 Napili Hau St.* ☎ 808/665-0222.

Crusted ahi with asparagus at Mama's Fish House.

Fresh seafood at the Pineapple Grill.

Lahaina Square, 840 Wainee St., Lahaina, ☎ 808/661-8883. Kamaole Beach Center, 2411 S. Kihei Rd., Kihei. Queen Kaahumnau Center, 275 Kaahumanu Ave., Kahului. ☎ 808/871-7726; www.mauitacos.com. Items range $4–$7.50. AE, DC, DISC, MC, V. Brunch, lunch & dinner daily. Map p 122.

★ Milagros Food Company

PAIA *SOUTHWESTERN/SEAFOOD* Sit outdoors and watch the parade of people, from tie-died hippies to ultra-chic Euro-trash, as you tuck in at this casual eatery. Great margaritas. *Hana Hwy. and Baldwin Ave.* ☎ 808/579-8755. Breakfast $6–$9; lunch $7–$12; dinner $14–$25. DC, MC, V. Breakfast, lunch & dinner daily. Map p 121.

★★ kids Moana Bakery & Cafe

PAIA *LOCAL/EUROPEAN* Paia's most creative cuisine, with Asian and European influences, highlights the menu at this quasi-stylish cafe. Entertainment 3 nights a week, ranges from jazz to Hawaiian to Latin. *71 Baldwin Ave.* ☎ 808/579-9999. Breakfast $7–$11; lunch $6–$13; dinner main courses $7–$29. MC, V. Breakfast, lunch & dinner Tues–Sun. Breakfast & lunch Mon. Map p 121.

kids Peggy Sue's

KIHEI *AMERICAN* This 1950s-style diner has oodles of charm (old-fashioned soda-shop stools and jukeboxes on every Formica table), you'll find sodas, shakes, floats, egg creams, and milkshakes, along with burgers, fries, and kids' meals for just $3.95. *Azeka Place II, 1279 S. Kihei Rd.* ☎ 808/875-8944. Burgers $7–$11; plate lunches $6–$12. AE, DISC, MC, V. Lunch & dinner daily. Map p 124.

★★★ Pineapple Grill Kapalua

KAPALUA *PACIFIC ISLAND* If you only had 1 night to eat on Maui this would be the place to go. Executive Chef Joey Macadangdang (a protégé of Roy Yamaguchi of Roy's Restaurant, see p 130) combines Asian/Filipino ingredients into culinary masterpieces. You'll dine overlooking the rolling hills of the Kapalua Golf Course. *200 Kapalua Dr.* ☎ 808/669-9600; www.pineapplekapalua.com. Lunch entrees $7–$17; dinner entrees $25–$35. AE, MC, V. Breakfast, lunch & dinner daily. Map p 123.

★ The Place

MAALAEA *ECLECTIC* In windy Maalaea Harbor, this elegant (wood floors, high ceilings, and ocean view) restaurant has a relaxing location and dishes ranging from

An entree at Roy's.

Sushi and sake at Sansei.

shrimp and goat cheese pizzas to seared fresh fish. *300 Maalaea Rd.* ☎ *808/243-2206. Lunch entrees $10–$15; dinner entrees $19–$26; pizzas $8–$12. MC. V. Lunch & dinner daily. Map p 124.*

★★ **Roy's Kahana Bar & Grill** KAHANA *EURO-ASIAN* One of Hawaii's most successful restaurants, Roy's has no dramatic view and is upstairs in a shopping mall. Yet the fabulous food packs 'em in every night. *Kahana Gateway Shopping Center, 4405 Honoapiilani Hwy.* ☎ *808/669-6999; www.roys restaurant.com. Main courses $14–$31. AE, DC, DISC, MC, V. Dinner daily. Map p 123.*

★★ **Sansei Seafood Restaurant and Sushi Bar** KAPALUA *PACIFIC RIM* Perpetual award-winner Sansei offers an extensive menu of Japanese and East–West delicacies, which are part Pacific Rim, part Hawaii Regional. *Office Rd.* ☎ *808/669-6286. Main courses $16–$38. AE, DISC, MC, V. Dinner daily. Also at Kihei Town Center, Kihei.* ☎ *808/879-0004. Map p 123.*

kids Shaka Sandwich & Pizza KIHEI *PIZZA* Award-winning pizzas, New York–style heroes, and Philly cheese steaks, calzones, salads, just-baked garlic bread, and home-made meatball sandwiches, all with fresh Maui produce. *1770 S. Kihei Rd.* ☎ *808/874-0331. Sandwiches $4.35–$11; pizzas $13–$26. No credit cards. Brunch, lunch & dinner daily. Map p 124.*

★ **kids Stella Blues Cafe** KIHEI *AMERICAN* There's something for everyone—vegetarians, kids, pasta, sandwich lovers, and hefty steak eaters—at this loud, lively, unpretentious eatery where Grateful Dead posters line the walls, and a covey of gleaming motorcycles is invariably parked outside. *Azeka II Shopping Center, 1279 S. Kihei Rd.* ☎ *808/874-3779. Main courses $8–$23. AE, DC, DISC, MC, V. Breakfast, lunch & dinner daily. Map p 124.*

★★ **Vino Italian Tapas & Wine Bar** KAPALUA *ITALIAN* Overlooking the rolling hills of the Kapalua Golf Course, this well-designed restaurant features small plates of exquisite Italian dishes that may inspire you to sing an aria. *Kapalua Village Course Golf Club House, Office Rd.* ☎ *808/661-VINO. Reservations recommended. Tapas $6–$18; large plates $19–$38. AE, DISC, MC, V. Lunch & dinner daily. Map p 123.*

★★ **kids The Waterfront at Maalaea** MAALAEA *SEAFOOD* The family-owned Waterfront has won many prestigious awards for service, the views, and, most of all, their just-caught seafood. *50 Hauoli St.* ☎ *808/244-9028; www.water frontrestaurant.net. Main courses $19–$38. AE, DC, DISC, MC, V. Dinner daily. Map p 124.* ●

Caprese salad at Vino Italian Tapas & Wine Bar.

Shopping Best Bets

Best **Alohawear**
★★★ Sig Zane Designs 53 Market St. (p 137)

Best **Asian Antiques**
★ Brown-Kobayashi 160-A N. Market St. (p 138)

Best **Hawaiian Antiques**
★★ Bird of Paradise Unique Antiques 56 N. Market St. (p 138)

Best **Place to Browse**
★★★ Bailey House Museum Gift Shop 2375-A Main St. (p 141)

Best **Local Maui Artists**
Hana Coast Gallery In the Hotel Hana-Maui (p 138)

Best **Cookies**
★★★ Broke Da Mouth Cookies 190 Alamaha St. (p 139)

Best **Gifts**
★ Maui Crafts Guild 43 Hana Hwy. (p 140)

Best **Gifts for the Kids**
★★ Maui Ocean Center 192 Maalaea Rd. (p 141)

Best for **Hawaiian CDs**
★★★ Totally Hawaiian Gift Gallery 1221 Honoapiilani Hwy. (p 141)

Best **Hand-blown Glass**
Ki'i Gallery The Shops at Wailea (p 142)

Best **High Fashion**
★★ Maggie Coulombe 505 Front St. (p 140)

Best **Place for a Lei**
Kmart 424 Dairy Rd. (p 140)

Best **Shoes**
Sandal Tree multiple locations (p 141)

Best **Shopping Mall**
Queen Kaahumanu Center 275 Kaahumanu Ave. (p 142)

Best **Sinfully Delicious Bakery**
★ T. Komoda Store and Bakery 3674 Baldwin Ave. (p 139)

Best **Souvenir to Ship Home**
★★ Sunrise Protea Haleakala Hwy/37. (p 140)

Best **Swimwear**
Lightning Bolt Maui 55 Kaahumanu Ave. (p 137)

Best **T-shirt Selection**
Crazy Shirts multiple locations (p 142)

The Maui Ocean Center has great gifts for kids.

Maui & Paia Shopping

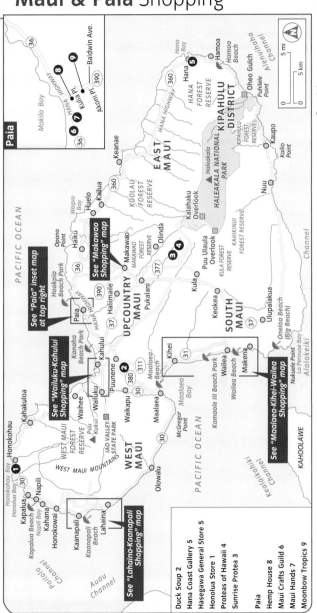

Paia

0   5 mi
0   5 km

Duck Soup 2
Hana Coast Gallery 5
Hasegawa General Store 5
Honolua Store 1
Proteas of Hawaii 4
Sunrise Protea 3

Paia
Hemp House 8
Maui Crafts Guild 6
Maui Hands 7
Moonbow Tropics 9

Lahaina & Kaanapali Shopping

Crazy Shirts (Lahaina) 6
Crazy Shirts (Lahaina Cannery Mall) 3
Crazy Shirts (Whaler's Village) 1
Crazy Shirts (Wharf Cinema) 8
Ki'i Gallery 2
Lahaina Arts Society Galleries 9
Lahaina Cannery Mall 3
Lahaina Center 4
Maggie Coulombe 10
The Old Lahaina Book Emporium 5
Paul Ropp (Whaler's Village) 1
Sandal Tree (Hyatt Regency Maui) 2
Sandal Tree (Whaler's Village) 1
Totally Hawaiian Gift Gallery
(Lahaina Cannery Mall) 3
Village Galleries in Lahaina 7
Whaler's Village 1

135

Wailuku & Kahului Shopping

Kahului
'Ano 'Ano Gallery and Gifts 8
Broke da Mouth Cookies 9
K-Mart 10
Lightning Bolt Maui 7
Maui County Store 8
Maui Mall 8
Queen Kaahumanu Center 6

Wailuku
Bailey House Museum Gift Shop 5
Bird of Paradise Unique Antiques 3
Brown-Kobayashi 2
Sandell 1
Sig Zane Designs 4

Maalaea/Kihei/Wailea Shopping

Crazy Shirts
(Piilani Village Shopping Center) 2

Crazy Shirts
(The Shops at Wailea) 3

CY Maui 3

Ki'i (Grand Wailea Resort) 4

Ki'i (The Shops at Wailea) 3

Maui Ocean Center 1

Nell 5

Sandal Tree 4

The Shops at Wailea 3

Makawao Shopping

0	1/10 mile
0	100 meters

Collections 7
Cuckoo for Coconuts 9
Gallery Maui 4
Holiday & Co. 8
Hui No'eau Visual
Arts Center 1
T. Komoda Store
and Bakery 6
Maui Hands 2
Sherri Reeve Gallery
and Gifts 5
Tropo 3

Makawao

MAUI

Maui Shopping A to Z

Alohawear
kids Lightning Bolt Maui Inc.
KAHULUI I love the excellent
selection of women's board shorts,
aloha shirts, swimwear, sandals,
and shoes, and all the necessary
accoutrements for fun in the sun.
55 Kaahumanu Ave. ☎ *808/877-3484.
AE, DC, MC, V. Map p 135.*

★★ Moonbow Tropics PAIA
I've found some top label aloha shirts
here. *36 Baldwin Ave.* ☎ *808/579-
8592. AE, DISC, MC, V. Map p 133.*

★★★ Sig Zane Designs WAILUKU
Do not miss this store where my
favorite Hawaiian designer sells
everything from the classic aloha
shirt, T-shirt, and golf shirt, to the

pareu, duffel bag, and muumuu.
53 Market St. ☎ *808/249-8997. AE,
MC, V. Map p 135.*

A display of Sig Zane shirts.

Tropo MAKAWAO A good stop for stylish men's aloha wear. *3643 Baldwin Ave.* ☎ *808/573-0356. AE, MC, V. Map p 137.*

Antiques & Collectibles
★★ Bird of Paradise Unique Antiques
WAILUKU I love wandering through the Hawaiiana nostalgia here. Items range from 1940s rattan furniture to vintage aloha shirts and classic Hawaiian music on cassettes. *56 N. Market St.* ☎ *808/242-7699. AE, MC, V. Map p 135.*

★ **Brown-Kobayashi** WAILUKU The focus is gracious living with Asian antiques. You'll find Japanese kimonos and obi, exotic Chinese woods, and more. *160-A N. Market St.* ☎ *808/242-0804. AE, MC, V. Map p 135.*

Duck Soup PUUNENE I've found terrific deals on jewelry, handbags, and art work at this virtually unknown warehouse full of Asian and Indonesian treasures. It's a bit out-of-the-way; call for directions. *Off Hwy. 311, about a mile from Puunene, near the Maui Animal Shelter and the Central Maui Baseyard.* ☎ *808/871-7875. MC, V. Map p 133.*

Art—Hawaiian
★ **'Ano 'Ano Gallery and Gifts** KAHULUI A real find for affordable art—from oil paintings to gold jewelry to carved wood. Some 50 Maui artists are represented. *Maui Mall, 70 E. Kaahumanu Ave.* ☎ *808/873-0233. AE, DC, DISC, MC, V. Map p 135.*

★★★ **Hana Coast Gallery** HANA If you only go to one gallery, make it this award-winning one devoted entirely to Hawaii's top artists (sculptures, paintings, prints, feather work, stonework, and carvings). It's Maui's best selection under one roof. *In the Hotel Hana-Maui.* ☎ *808/248-8636. AE, MC, V. Map p 133.*

★★ **Hui No'eau Visual Arts Center** MAKAWAO I can spend hours wandering the gift shop, which features many one-of-a-kind local works. *2841 Baldwin Ave.* ☎ *808/572-6560; www.huinoeau. com. AE, DISC, MC, V. Map p 137.*

Gallery Maui MAKAWAO Pop in to see the quality of work by Maui artists, from Norfolk pine bowls to watercolors. *3643-A Baldwin Ave.* ☎ *808/572-8092. AE, DC, MC, V. Map p 137.*

Ki'i Gallery KAANAPALI, WAILEA This shop features glass in all forms, from handblown vessels to jewelry. I can't pass by without stopping to browse. *In the Hyatt Regency Maui, 200 Nohea Kai Dr.* ☎ *808/661-4456. Map p. 134. Also at the Grand Wailea Resort,* ☎ *808/874-3059, Map p. 136. The Shops at Wailea,* ☎ *808/874-1181. AE, DC, DISC, MC, V. Map p 136.*

Glass display at Ki'i Gallery.

A painting at the Sherri Reeve Gallery.

★ **Lahaina Arts Society Galleries** LAHAINA   Changing monthly exhibits of the Maui artist-members range from paintings to fiber art, to ceramics, sculpture, prints, jewelry, and more. "Art in the Park" fairs are every second and fourth weekend of the month. *648 Wharf St.* ☎ *808/ 661-3228. MC, V. Map p 134.*

★ **Sherri Reeve Gallery and Gifts** MAKAWAO   If you want to take a bit of the vibrant color and feel of the islands home with you, stop by this open-air gallery that sells everything from inexpensive cards, hand-painted tiles, and T-shirts to original works and limited editions. *3669 Baldwin Ave.* ☎ *808/572-8931; www.sreeve.com. AE, DISC, MC, V. Map p 137.*

Village Galleries in Lahaina. LAHAINA   The oldest continuously operated gallery on Maui is known among art collectors as a showcase for regional artists. *120 and 180 Dickenson St.* ☎ *808/661-4402 or 808/661-5559. Also at the Ritz-Carlton Kapalua, 1 Ritz-Carlton Dr.* ☎ *808/669-1800.*

Bookstores
The Old Lahaina Book Emporium LAHAINA   Chockablock with 25,000 used books in stacks, shelves, counters, and aisles, this bookstore is a browser's dream. It has great books on Hawaii. *834 Front St.* ☎ *808/661-1399.*

Edibles
★★★ **kids Broke da Mouth Cookies** KAHULUI   This store is my weakness: terrific cookies ($3.25 a bag), ranging from chocolate mac-nut, oatmeal raisin, and shortbread to almond, peanut butter, and coconut crunch. So good, you'll eat them long before you get home. *190 Alamaha St.* ☎ *808/873-9255. No cards. Map p 135.*

★ **kids T. Komoda Store and Bakery** MAKAWAO   Get here early before their famous cream puffs are sold out; also check out the delicious cinnamon rolls, dough-nuts, pies, and chocolate cake. *3674 Baldwin Ave.* ☎ *808/572-7261. No cards. Map p 137.*

Fashion
CY Maui WAILEA   Women looking for washable, flowing clothing in silks, rayons, and natural fibers will love this shop. *In The Shops at Wailea, 3750 Wailea Alanui Dr, A-30.* ☎ *808/ 891-0782. AE, MC, V. Map p 136.*

★ **Collections** MAKAWAO   One of my favorites, this eclectic shop is filled with spirited clothing reflecting the ease and color of island living. *3677 Baldwin Ave.* ☎ *808/572-0781. MC, V. Map p 137.*

Hemp House PAIA   A surprisingly great selection of clothing and acces-sories made of hemp (jeans, linen-like pants, dresses, shirts, and so on), a sturdy, eco-friendly, and sensible fiber. *16 Baldwin Ave.* ☎ *808/579-8880. AE, DISC, MC, V. Map p 133.*

★ **Holiday & Co.** MAKAWAO   I love to just wander around this tiny store checking out the collection of surprisingly attractive natural fiber women's clothing, ranging from easygoing dresses to shawls, even a few aloha shirts. *3681 Baldwin Ave.* ☎ *808/572-1470. AE, DC, DISC, MC, V. Map p 137.*

★★ **Maggie Coulombe** LAHAINA
I cannot resist this high-fashion
store with Maggie Coulombe's latest
couture, jersey, linen, pareo, and
shoes, plus accessories, jewelry,
and a few surprises. *505 Front St.*
☎ *808/662-0696; www.maggie
coulombe.com. AE, DC, DISC, MC, V.
Map p 134.*

★ **Nell** WAILEA   Top labels and
elegant clothing are the stars here.
Fairmont Kea Lani Hotel. ☎ *808/
875-4100, ext. 390. AE, MC, V.
Map p 136.*

Paul Ropp KAANAPALI   The Bali
fashion designer's only store outside of Indonesia features his lively,
colorful, and eccentric style of
dressing, which is perfect for
Maui's tropical climate. *In Whalers
Village, 2435 Kaanapali Pkwy.*
☎ *808/661-8000. AE, DISC, MC, V.
Map p 134.*

Flowers & Lei
Kmart KAHULUI   I've scoured the
island and, surprisingly, this chain
store has some of the most unusual
and outstanding leis on Maui at very
moderate prices. *424 Dairy Rd.*
☎ *808/871-8553. AE, DISC, MC, V.
Map p 135.*

★★ **Sunrise Protea** KULA   Send
these other-worldly flowers back
home to your friends—not only will
they survive shipping anywhere in
the world, but your pals will be
astounded and amazed. *Haleakala
Hwy./37.* ☎ *808/876-0200; www.
sunriseprotea.com. AE, DISC, MC, V.
Map p 133.*

Proteas of Hawaii KULA   In
addition to flowers, they offer regular walking tours of the University of
Hawaii Extension Service gardens
across the street. *417 Mauna Pl.*
☎ *808/878-2533; www.proteasof
hawaii.com. MC, V. Map p 133.*

The interior of Maggie Coulombe.

General Stores
★★ **Hasegawa General Store**
HANA   I love this old-fashioned
store, where the aisles are choked
with merchandise from groceries to
every tape and CD that mentions
Hana, and even T-shirts and beach
toys. *Hana Hwy., in Hana.* ☎ *808/
248-8231. AE, MC, V. Map p 133.*

★★ **Honolua Store** KAPALUA
For the best prices in a pricey resort
area, this is my favorite place to get
every day essentials, clothing, even
budget-priced deli items. *502 Office
Rd.* ☎ *808/669-6128. AE, DC, DISC,
MC, V. Map p 133.*

Hawaiian Gifts
Cuckoo for Coconuts
MAKAWAO   A sense of humor per-
vades every item here, from vintage
collectibles, gag gifts, and silly
coconuts, to 1960s and 1970s aloha
wear, tutus, sequined dresses, vintage wedding gowns, and all sorts
of other oddities. *1158 Makawao
Ave.* ☎ *808/573-6887.*

★ **Maui Crafts Guild** PAIA
The high quality and unique artwork
at this artist-owned and -operated
guild, encompasses everything from
pit-fired raku to hand-painted fabrics,
jewelry, beadwork, traditional Hawaiian stonework, even banana bark
paintings. *43 Hana Hwy.* ☎ *808/
579-9697. AE, MC, V. Map p 133.*

Maui Hands MAKAWAO, PAIA
Great Hawaiian gifts can be found at
this store, where 90% of the items
are made by Maui artists and sold at
prices that aren't inflated. *Courtyard,
3620 Baldwin Ave.* ☎ *808/572-5194.
Map p. 133. 84 Hana Hwy.* ☎ *808/
579-9245. AE, MC, V. Map p 133.*

**★★★ kids Totally Hawaiian Gift
Gallery** LAHAINA I have spent
hours browsing here, checking out
everything from Niihau shell jewelry,
to excellent Hawaiian CDs, and many
things Hawaiian (carved wood bowls,
Hawaiian quilts, handcrafted dolls,
and koa works of art). *Lahaina
Cannery Mall, 1221 Honoapiilani
Hwy.* ☎ *808/667-2558. AE, DC, DISC,
MC, V. Map p 134.*

Museum Stores
**★★★ Bailey House Museum
Gift Shop** WAILUKU For made-in-
Hawaii items, this small shop is a
must-stop. The selection of remark-
able gift items includes Hawaiian
music, exquisite woods, traditional
Hawaiian games, pareus, books,
lauhala hats, hand-sewn pheasant
hatbands, jams and jellies, Maui
cookbooks, and an occasional Hawaiian quilt. *Bailey House Museum Shop,
2375-A Main St.* ☎ *808/244-3326.
MC, V. Map p 135.*

★★ kids Maui Ocean Center
MAALAEA Stop here for plush
stuffed marine animals; nature
books; T-shirts; and an array of fine
artwork, jewelry, and Hawaiiana created by some of the island's most
prominent artists. *Maalaea Harbor
Village, 192 Maalaea Rd. (the triangle between Honoapiilani Hwy. and
Maalaea Rd.).* ☎ *808/270-7000. AE,
DISC, MC, V. Map p 136.*

Shoes
★★★ Sandal Tree KAANAPALI,
WAILEA My fave store for sandals,
ranging from rubber thongs, athletic

shoes, and Top-Siders to dressy
pumps, designer footwear, hats, and
much more. Prices are realistic too.
*In Whalers Village, 2435 Kaanapali
Pkwy.* ☎ *808/667-5330. Map p 134.
Also in Grand Wailea Resort, 3850
Wailea Alanui Dr., Wailea (*☎ *808/
874-9006). Map p 136. Also in Hyatt
Regency Maui, 200 Nohea Kai Dr.
(*☎ *808/661-3495). AE, MC, V. Map
p 136.*

Shopping Centers
Lahaina Cannery Mall LAHAINA
This former pineapple cannery is
now a maze of shops and restaurants. Check out **Sir Wilfred's Coffee House,** where you can unwind
with espresso and croissants. *1221
Honoapiilani Hwy., Lahaina.* ☎ *808/
661-5304. Map p 134.*

Lahaina Center LAHAINA Still a
work in progress, this mall has easy
access to more than 30 shops, a
salon, restaurants, a nightclub, and
a four-plex movie-theater complex.
900 Front St. ☎ *808/667-9216. Map
p 134.*

Maui Mall KAHULUI This is a
place of everyday shopping with
stores like Long's Drugs and Star

*A fish plate at the Maui Ocean Center's
gift shop.*

The Best Shopping

Market. Worth checking out are **'Ano 'Ano Gallery and Gifts** (p 138), and **Maui County Store** (below). Don't miss **Tasaka Guri Guri**, a decades-old purveyor of icy treats. *70 E. Kaahumanu Ave.* ☎ 808/877-7559. Map p 135.

★ **kids Queen Kaahumanu Center** KAHULUI Offers more than 100 shops, restaurants, and theaters. Kaahumanu covers all the bases, from arts and crafts to a **Foodland Supermarket**. *275 Kaahumanu Ave.* ☎ 808/877-3369. Map p 135.

★ **The Shops at Wailea** WAILEA This collection of high-end shops sells expensive souvenirs, gifts, clothing, and accessories. The chains rule, but dedicated shoppers can still find some more unusual options. My picks include: **Na Hoku**, *the* place to go for creative, distinctive jewelry with an island touch; and **Ki`i Gallery**, which houses one of Hawaii's most comprehensive collections of fine art from glass to original paintings. *3750 Wailea*

Calla lily vases at Ki`i Gallery.

Alanui. ☎ 808/891-6770; www.shops atwailea.com.

Whaler's Village KAANAPALI I find upscale Whalers Village disappointing. Although it offers everything from Prada to Ferragamo, it's short on local shops, and parking at the nearby lot is expensive. The only stores I recommend are: **Lahaina Printsellers, Cinnamon Girl,** and **Paul Ropp** (p 140). *2435 Kaanapali Pkwy.* ☎ 808/661-4567. Map p 134.

T-shirts

★★ **Crazy Shirts** VARIOUS LOCATIONS Confession: a huge portion of my wardrobe consists of Crazy Shirts T-shirts. These 100% cotton T-shirts not only last for years, they also make perfect souvenirs and gifts. *Multiple locations: Whalers Village,* ☎ 808/661-0117, Map p 134; 865 Front St., ☎ 808/661-4775, Map p 134; Wharf Cinema, ☎ 808/ 661-4712, Map p 134; Piilani Village Shopping Center, ☎ 808/875-6440, Map p 136; Lahaina Cannery Mall, ☎ 808/661-4788, Map p 134; Shops at Wailea, ☎ 808/875-6435, Map p 136. AE, DISC, MC, V.

kids Maui County Store KAHULUI Here's your chance to get official Maui County Police and Fire logo T-shirts and other Maui County logo shirts, plus logo wear from the University of Hawaii. Prices are wallet-friendly. *Maui Mall, 70 Kaahumanu Ave.,* ☎ 808/877-6669; www. mauicountystore.com. DC, MC, V. Map p 135.

Sandell WAILUKU If you want the inside scoop on Maui politics as well as some social commentary, stop by and chat with artist/illustrator/cartoonist David Sandell, who has been commenting on Maui since the early 1970s through this art work. Also check out his inexpensive T-shirts. *133 Market St.* ☎ 808/249-0234. No cards. Map p 135. ●

Nightlife & Performing Arts
Best Bets

Best Place to Bury Your Toes in the Sand
★ Leilani's/Hula Grill *Whaler's Village* (p 148)

Best for Hawaiian Music
★★ Hapa's Night Club *41 E. Lipoa St.* (p 148)

Best Dance Floor
★ Tsunami Nightclub *Grand Wailea Beach Hotel* (p 149)

Best Place to Drink with Locals
★ Kahului Ale House *355 E. Kamehameha Ave.* (p 148)

Best Family Show
★★★ kids Kupanaha *Kaanapali Beach Hotel* (p 149)

Best Music
★★ kids Moanai Bakery & Café *71 Baldwin Ave.* (p 149)

Best Hawaiian Slack-Key Music
★★★ kids Masters of Hawaiian Slack-Key Guitar Series *Ritz-Carlton Kapalua* (p 150)

Best Hotel Lounge
★ Four Seasons Lobby Lounge *Four Seasons Wailea* (p 148)

Best Luau
★★★ kids Old Lahaina Luau *1251 Front St.* (p 150)

Best Performing Arts Center
★★★ Maui Arts and Cultural Center *1 Cameron Way* (p 149)

Best for Big Name Musicians
★★ Casanova *1188 Makawao Ave.* (p 148)

Best Show
★★★ kids 'Ulalena *878 Front St.* (p 149)

Best for Movies
★★★ Maui Film Festival *Wailea Golf Course* (p 148)

Enjoy a cocktail with your Maui sunset.

Sunset Cocktails

At the southern end of Lahaina, in the 505 Front St. complex, **Pacific'o** (☎ 808/667-4341) is a solid hit, with a raised bar, seating on the ocean, and a backdrop of Lanai across the channel. A few steps away sister restaurant **I'o** shares the same vista, with an appetizer menu and a techno-curved bar that will wow you as much as the drop-dead-gorgeous view.

In Wailea, the restaurants at the new Shops at Wailea, 3750 Wailea Alanui, including highly successful **Tommy Bahama** (☎ 808/875-9983) and **Longhi's** (☎ 808/891-8883), are a noteworthy addition to the sunset scene.

Casanova 3
Masters of Hawaiian Slack Key
Guitar Series 1
Moana Bakery & Café 2

Wailuku - Kahului
Iao Theater 4
Kahului Ale House 7
Mañana Garage 6
Maui Arts and Cultural Center 5

Lahaina & Kaanapali Nightlife

Cheeseburger in Paradise 7
Feast at Lele 8
Hard Rock Café 4
Kupanaha 1
Leilani's/Hula Grill 2
Longhi's 5
Maui Brews 4
Old Lahaina Luau 3
'Ulalena 6
Warren & Annabelle's 4

Kihei & Wailea Nightlife

Four Season's Lobby Lounge 4
Hapa's Night Club 1
Sports Page Bar 2
Tsunami Nightclub 3

Maui Nightlife A to Z

Bars & Cocktail Lounges

★★ **Casanova** MAKAWAO Expect good blues, rock 'n' roll, reggae, jazz, Hawaiian, and the top names in local and visiting entertainment. I love the Sunday afternoon live jazz from 3 to 6pm. *1188 Makawao Ave.* ☎ *808/ 572-0220. Map p 145.*

Cheeseburger in Paradise LAHAINA Loud, live tropical rock blasts into the streets and out to sea nightly from 4:30 to 11pm. *Front/Lahainaluna Sts.* ☎ *808/ 661-4855. Map p 146.*

★ **Four Seasons Lobby Lounge** WAILEA For a quiet evening with gentle jazz or soft Hawaiian music, sink into the plush furniture and order an exotic drink. Nightly live music from 8:30 to 11:30pm. *Four Seasons Wailea.* ☎ *808/874-8000. Map p 147.*

★★ **Hapa's Night Club** KIHEI When I'm hungry for the sweet sounds of Hawaiian music, I give Hapa's a call to see who's on for the night. *41 E. Lipoa St.* ☎ *808/ 879-9001. Map p 147.*

Hard Rock Cafe LAHAINA Occasional live music, but mainly DJs entertain at this loud, 20-something scene. *900 Front St.* ☎ *808/667-7400. Map p 146.*

★ **Kahului Ale House** KAHULUI Locals gather here for karaoke and live music. A DJ spins on Saturday from 10pm. *355 E. Kamehameha Ave.* ☎ *808/877-9001. Map p 145.*

★ **Leilani's/Hula Grill** KAANAPALI Both oceanfront restaurants have busy, upbeat bars and tables on the sand. Hula Grill's Barefoot Bar appetizer menu is a cut above Leilani's. Leilani's has live music daily from 3:30 to 6pm, while at Hula Grill the happy hour starts at 3pm and the live music at 6pm. *Whaler's Village, Leilani's* ☎ *808/661-4495. Hula Grill* ☎ *808/667-6636. Map p 146.*

Longhi's LAHAINA Live salsa or jazz spills out into the streets from 9:30pm on weekends. I love people-watching here. It's a real mix, everyone from Midwestern tourists to the occasional rock star. *888 Front St.* ☎ *808/667-2288. Map p 146.*

★★ **kids** **Mañana Garage** KAHULUI This eclectic family restaurant attracts a crowd in their 30s and 40s with live music Wednesday through Saturday nights, from 6:30pm. *33 Lono Ave.* ☎ *808/873-0220. Map p 145.*

Maui Brews LAHAINA A young, hip crowd comes to this late-night restaurant-turned nightclub after

Maui Movie Magic

If you are headed to Maui, try to plan your trip around the **Maui Film Festival** (☎ 808/579-9244; www.mauifilmfestival.com), which always starts the Wednesday before Father's Day in June. The 5-day festival premiers nightly films in the **Celestial Cinema,** an under-the-stars, open-air "outdoor theater" on the Wailea Golf Course, which features a 50-foot-wide screen in Dolby Digital Surround Sound.

Enjoy movies under the stars in the Celestial Cinema.

9pm, for the swing, salsa, reggae, and jams—either live or with a DJ. *900 Front St.* ☎ *808/667-7794. Map p 146.*

★★ **kids Moanai Bakery & Café** PAIA   This retro restaurant is my favorite place to relax. Bring the entire family for the Vintage Hawaiian 6:30 to 9pm on Wednesday; smooth jazz and hot blues 6:30 to 9pm on Friday; and flamingo guitar and gypsy violin 6 to 9pm on Sunday. *71 Baldwin Ave.* ☎ *808/579-9999. Map p 145.*

Sports Page Bar KIHEI   This crowded, typical sports bar features live music Monday through Saturday from 9pm. *2411 S. Kihei Rd.* ☎ *808/ 879-0602. Map p 147.*

★ **Tsunami Nightclub** WAILEA A mixed-age clientele flocks to this crowded dance floor that offers a DJ's selection on Friday and Saturday 9:30pm to 2am. *Grand Wailea Beach Hotel.* ☎ *808/875-1234. Map p 147.*

Dance, Theater & Shows

Iao Theater WAILUKU   It's not Broadway, but Maui does have live community theater, ranging from locally written productions to well-known plays and musicals. *68 N. Market St.,* ☎ *808/244-8680 or 808/242-6969 for box office and program information. www.mauion stage.com. Map p 145.*

★★★ **kids Kupanaha** KAANAPALI This dinner show for the entire family, which features magic, illusions,

and the story of the Hawaii fire goddess, Pele, gets my vote for a great family outing. Tuesday through Saturday from 5 to 8pm. *Kaanapali Beach Hotel.* ☎ *808/661-0011; www.kbhmaui.com. Tickets (which include dinner) $75–$85 adults, $49 teens (ages 13–20), and $35 for children ages 6 to 12 (free for children 5 and under). Map p 146.*

★★★ **Maui Arts and Cultural Center** KAHULUI   This is a first-class center for the visual and performing arts. Bonnie Raitt has performed here, as have Pearl Jam, Ziggy Marley, Tony Bennett, the American Indian Dance Theatre, the Maui Symphony Orchestra, and Jonny Lang, not to mention the finest in local talent. The center has a visual-arts gallery, an outdoor amphitheater, and two theaters. *1 Cameron Way.* ☎ *808/242-7469; www.mauiarts.org. Ticket prices vary. Map p 145.*

★★★ **kids 'Ulalena** LAHAINA   The whole family will be riveted by this incredible show which weaves Hawaiian mythology with drama, dance, and state-of-the-art multimedia. The cast performs Polynesian dance, original music, acrobatics, and chant in an interactive experience that often leaves the audience breathless. *Maui Myth and Magic Theatre, 878 Front St.* ☎ *877/688-4800 or 808/661-9913; www.ulalena.com. Tues–Sat 6:30pm. Tickets: $50–$70 adults; $30–$50 for children ages 12 and under. Map p 146.*

Maui Arts and Cultural Center.

★ Warren & Annabelle's

LAHAINA   This unusual magic/comedy cocktail show stars illusionist Warren Gibson and "Annabelle," a ghost from the 1800s. She plays the grand piano as Warren dazzles you with his sleight-of-hand magic. *900 Front St.* ☎ *808/667-6244; www. warrenandannabelles.com. Tickets: $50. Map p 146.*

Hawaiian Music

★★★ kids Masters of Hawaiian Slack-Key Guitar Series

KAPALUA   For a chance to see a side of Hawaii that few visitors do, come to this Tuesday night production, where host George Kahumoku, Jr. introduces a new slack-key master every week. Not only is there incredible Hawaiian music and singing, but George and his guest "talk story" about old Hawaii, music, and Hawaiian culture. *Ritz-Carlton Kapalua.* ☎ *808/669-3858; www.slackkey.com. Tickets: $40. Map p 145.*

Luau

★★★ kids Old Lahaina Luau

LAHAINA   This is the best luau on Maui—perhaps in the entire state. The luau begins at sunset and

Entertainment at the Old Lahaina Luau.

features Tahitian and Hawaiian entertainment, including ancient hula, modern hula, and an intelligent narrative on the dance's rocky course of survival into modern times. The entertainment is riveting. The food, served from an open-air thatched structure, is as much Pacific Rim as Hawaiian, and mixes in some well-known western favorites. If you have been here, then be sure to see **The Feast at Lele** (p 126). *1251 Front St.* ☎ *800/248-5828 or 808/667-1998; www.oldlahainaluau.com. Tickets: $89 adults; $59 children 12 and under. Map p 146.* ●

Slack-key master and two-time Grammy winner, Keoki Kahumoku.

The Best of Lanai **in One Day**

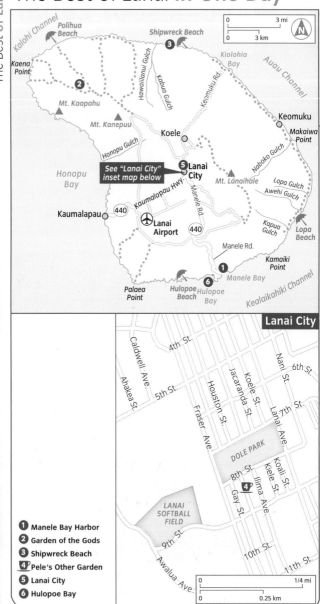

Lanai City

1 Manele Bay Harbor
2 Garden of the Gods
3 Shipwreck Beach
4 Pele's Other Garden
5 Lanai City
6 Hulopoe Bay

The smallest of all the Hawaiian islands, Lanai was once a big pineapple plantation. Today it is home to two exclusive resorts, hundreds of years of history, one small town, and some of the friendliest people you will ever meet. It's possible to get an overview of this island in a single day: If you catch the first ferry, departing at 6:45am, you can see all my favorite spots (the island's unusual "supernatural" site, a windswept beach that's perfect for beach-combing, and quaint Lanai City), plus get in some beach time and still make it back to Lahaina in time for dinner. START: **Manele Bay Harbor. Trip Length: 68 miles (109.4km)**

1 Manele Bay Harbor. To make the most of your day on Lanai, take the first ferry, which leaves at 6:45am. Seeing the morning sunlight glinting off the ocean is one of my favorite ways to start the day. Small, picturesque Manele Bay Harbor has a handful of boats ranging from old fishing vessels to luxury high-tech yachts. If you've already arranged a 4-wheel-drive rental through the ferry company (see p 155), they'll pick you up at the harbor and take you to the car-rental company in Lanai City, a 30- to 40-minute trip.

From the car-rental company, it's another 14 miles (22.5km) to the Garden of the Gods. Turn right onto Lanai Ave., then right (north) again to Hwy. 430 (Keomuku Hwy.). Turn left on Poliha Rd., just behind the stables and before the tennis courts (look for the rock sign "Garden of the Gods"). Allow about 25 minutes.

2 ★★ **kids Garden of the Gods.** Allow about 15 minutes to explore this rugged, barren, beautiful place on Lanai's north shore. You'll arrive early in the morning, when the light casts eerie shadows on these mysterious lava formations. Strewn by volcanic forces, the rocks are a brilliant mix of reds, oranges, ochers, and yellows. Ancient Hawaiians considered this desolate, windswept place supernatural. Scientists, however, have other, less colorful explanations. Some call the area an "ongoing posterosional event"; others say it's just "plain and simple badlands."

Manele Bay Harbor.

Garden of the Gods.

Retrace your steps to Hwy. 430 (Keomuku Hwy.) and turn left. Continue down the steep switchback to the ocean. Turn left and drive to the end of the road. Allow 60 minutes to drive these 20 miles (32.2km) on windy, dirt roads.

3 ★ kids Shipwreck Beach. This 8-mile- (12.9km-) long windswept strand on Lanai's northeastern shore—named for the rusty ship *Liberty* stuck on the coral reef—is a sailor's nightmare and a beachcomber's dream. The swimming isn't great here, nor is the snorkeling (too murky), but this is the best place in Hawaii to beachcomb. Strong currents yield all sorts of flotsam, from Japanese handblown-glass fish floats and rare pelagic paper nautilus shells to lots of junk. From December to April,

when the Pacific humpbacks cruise in from Alaska, this is also a great place to spot whales. Plan to spend about an hour.

It will take about 45 minutes to retrace your route back up Hwy. 430, into Lanai City, 12 miles (19.3km) away. Continue down Lanai Ave., turn right on Eighth Ave., just after Dole Square. Park next to the Square on Eighth across from Houston St.

4 ★★ kids Pele's Other Garden. This deli and bistro is a good lunch spot. You can take out, but I love to order one of their wraps and sit outside under one of the umbrellas, watching the goings on in the town square. See p 160.

5 ★★ kids Lanai City. Perched at 1,645 feet (493.5m) above sea level, almost at the dead-center of the island, sits this old-fashioned town centered on Dole Square. Built in 1924, this plantation village is a tidy grid of quaint tin-roofed cottages in bright pastels, with tropical gardens of banana, *lilikoi*, and papaya. The charming village square is lined with towering Norfolk and Cook Island pines and plantation buildings housing a couple of general stores selling basic necessities, a smattering of restaurants, an art

Pele's Other Garden.

Hulopoe Beach.

gallery, an art center, and a whimsical shop. A few blocks over is a post office and a coffee shop that outshines any Starbucks. Give yourself an hour or 2 to mosey from one shop to the next.

Continue down 8th Ave. to Fraser Ave. and turn left. Go right at Hwy. 440 (Kaumalapau Hwy.). Turn left at Manele Rd., where Hwy. 440 continues. Continue to the end at Hulopoe Beach Park. Allow 30 to 35 minutes for the 11-mile (17.7km) trip.

6 ★★★ kids Hulopoe Beach. This wide beach is one of my favorites in the entire state. Not only is it a terrific snorkeling spot (especially along the rocks to your left as you face the ocean), but it is a marine preserve, where taking of fish or other marine critters is forbidden. Boats cannot anchor in the bay, so you have the entire ocean to yourself.

Take the 5-minute walk from Hulopoe Beach Park to Manele Bay to catch the last ferry back to Lahaina at 6:45pm.

Getting To & Around Lanai

There are no direct flights from the Mainland to Lanai; you'll have to make a connection in Honolulu or Kahului (on Maui), where you catch a plane for the 25-minute flight to Lanai's airport. Twin-engine planes are the only air service to Lanai. **Island Air** (☎ 800/652-6541 or 808/565-6744; www.islandair.com) offers six flights a day from Honolulu and one direct flight from Maui.

Another option is a round-trip on **Expeditions Lahaina/Lanai Passenger Ferry** (☎ 808/661-3756; www.go-lanai.com), which costs $52 adults round-trip and $42 children. The ferry runs five times daily between Lahaina and Lanai's Manele Bay Harbor. The 9-mile (14.5km) channel crossing takes 45 minutes to an hour, depending on sea conditions. Reservations are strongly recommended. Baggage is limited to two checked bags and one carry-on.

I recommend renting a 4-wheel-drive vehicle to use on the island. (Lanai only has 30 miles/48.3km of paved roads, and hundreds of miles of unpaved roads.) You can book through Expeditions Ferry; the $176 rental fee includes a round-trip ferry ticket for one.

The Best of Lanai **in Three Days**

Day 1
1 Polihua Beach
2 Garden of the Gods
3 Kanepuu Preserve
4 Lanai City
5 Henry Clay's Rotisserie

Day 2
6 Blue Ginger Café
7 Hulopoe Beach
7A Pool Grille
7B Ihilani

Day 3
8A Munro Trail
8B The Challenge at Manele
8C The Experience at Koele
8D Hulopoe Court

Where to Stay
7A Four Seasons Resort at Manele Bay
5 Hotel Lanai
8D The Lodge at Koele

Where to Dine
6 Blue Ginger Café
5 Henry Clay's Rotisserie
7B Ihilani
7A Ocean Grill
9 Pele's Other Garden

Three days is ideal for Lanai. This is enough time to explore the island one day, relax on the beach the next, and have a more active last day, either hiking to the top of the island, indulging in some of Hawaii's best scuba diving and snorkeling, or teeing off on one of Lanai's two resort golf courses. START: **Lanai City. Trip Length: 85 miles (136.9km)**

Travel Tips

See the box on p 155 for information on getting to and around Lanai. Generally you will not need a car if you are staying at one of the two resorts or at the Hotel Lanai (they provide shuttle bus service), but exploring Lanai's many back roads is a fantastic opportunity to go four-wheeling. Make sure to grab a picnic lunch from **Pele's Other Garden** (p 160) before you head out of Lanai City.

Go north on Lanai Ave., then right on Hwy. 430 (Keomuku Hwy.). Turn left on Poliha Rd., just behind the stables and before the tennis courts (look for the rock sign "Garden of the Gods"). The next 26 miles (41.9km) is on dirt jeep trails and will take 60 to 75 minutes all the way down to the beach.

1 ★★ kids **Polihua Beach.** Lanai's largest white-sand beach is a great spot to begin your journey.

The beach's strong currents are generally not safe for swimming, and it can be windy, but the beach will probably be deserted and you'll have a great view of Molokai in the distance. So many sea turtles once hauled themselves out of the water to lay their eggs in the sun-baked sand on Lanai's northwestern shore that Hawaiians named the beach here *Polihua*, or "egg nest." Although the endangered green sea turtles are making a comeback, they're seldom seen here now. You're more likely to spot an offshore whale (in season) or the perennial litter that washes up onto this deserted beach. There are no facilities, so bring water and sunscreen. Relax for a couple of hours, eat lunch, and walk the beach looking for shells.

Retrace your route back on Polihua Rd. about 12 miles (19.3km) and 45 minutes.

2 ★★ kids **Garden of the Gods.** See p 153 **2**.

Polihua Beach.

A sign in Lanai City.

Continue another 5 miles (8km) on Polihua Rd.

❸ ★ kids Kanepuu Preserve.
Stop and take this self-guided nature trail, about a 10- to 15-minute walk through eight stations, with interpretive signs explaining the natural or cultural significance of what you're seeing. Kanepuu is one of the last remaining examples of the type of forest that once covered the dry lowlands throughout the state. There are some 49 plant species here that are found only in Hawaii.

Retrace your steps back to Lanai City.

❹ ★★ kids Lanai City. See p 154
❺ for a description of this tiny village.

Plan to have dinner at an old fashioned country lodge dining room, **5' ★ kids Henry Clay's Rotisserie.** My favorites are the Rajun Cajun Clay's shrimp, a fiery concoction of hefty shrimp in a spiced tomato broth, and the "Almost Grandma's Gumbo," both straight from Chef Henry's New Orleans roots. See p 160.

Start your second day with breakfast at tiny **6' Blue Ginger Café;** my favorite is the homemade French toast. Order a second cup of coffee and sit and chat awhile with the locals; introduce yourself and ask them questions about Lanai. See p 160.

From Lanai City take Hwy. 440 (Kaumalapau Hwy.). Turn left at Manele Rd., where Hwy. 440 continues. Continue to the end at Hulupoe Beach Park. Allow 30 to 35 minutes for the 11-mile (17.7km) trip.

❼ ★★★ kids Hulopoe Beach.
For your second day, plan to laze around Hulopoe Beach. Bring a good book, watch the kids play in the surf, or take a long slow walk around the crescent-shaped bay. Wander over to the Four Seasons–Lanai at Manele Bay for lunch poolside at the **7A ★ kids Pool Grille** (p 160), where the yummy calamari salad with crispy chow mein noodles is "onolicious," as we say in Hawaii. Splurge on dinner: Book a table at **7B Ihilani** (p 160), with a view of the sun sinking into the ocean and indulge in the exquisite Italian cuisine (I recommend the ahi caponata with eggplant). Be sure to save room for dessert.

Those wanting to hike or drive the Munro Trail, the well-marked trail begins at Lanai Cemetery along Keomoku Rd. (Hwy. 430). If you are interested in taking the Trilogy sail-snorkel, the boat leaves from Manele Boat Harbor (From Lanai City take Hwy. 440/Kaumalapau Hwy., and continue to the end of the road. Allow 30–35 minutes for the 11-mile/17.7km trip.) The Experience at Koele Golf Course is next door to the Lodge at Koele in Lanai City; and the Challenge at Manele is

next door to the Four Seasons–
Lanai at Manele Bay.

**⑧ Adventures on Land or
Water.** On your third day, if it hasn't
been raining and the ground is dry,
do a little exploring. Here are a few
options: The truly ambitious can
spend the day (plan on at least 7 hr.)
climbing to the top of Lanai at Lanaihale on the ★★★ **⑧A Munro Trail.**
This tough, 11-mile (17.7km) (round-
trip) uphill climb through groves of
Norfolk pines begins at Lanai Cemetery along Keomoku Road (Hwy.
430). It's a lung-buster, but if you
reach the top, you'll be rewarded
with a breathtaking view of Molokai,
Maui, Kahoolawe, the peaks of the
Big Island, and—on a really clear
day—Oahu in the distance. The trail
follows Lanai's ancient caldera rim,
ending up at the island's highest
point, Lanaihale. Go in the morning
for the best visibility. After 4 miles
(6.4km), you'll get a view of Lanai
City. If you're tired, you can retrace
your steps from here, otherwise,
continue the last 1¼ miles (2km) to
the top. Diehards can head down
Lanai's steep south-crater rim to join
the highway to Manele Bay. Pencil in

a soak in a hot tub on your return. If
you'd rather go out on (or into) the
water, contact ★★★ **kids Trilogy
Lanai Ocean Sports** (☎ 888/
MAUI-800; www.visitlanai.com)
about their sailing/snorkeling,
whale-watching, or scuba trips.
Golfers can head for either the **⑧B**
★★★ **The Challenge at Manele**
(next to the Four Seasons–Lanai at
Manele in Hulopoe Bay, ☎ 800/
321-4666; greens fees $225 or $190
for resort guests), a target-style,
desert-links course, designed by
Jack Nicklaus, and one of the most
challenging in the state; or **⑧C** ★★
The Experience at Koele (The
Lodge at Koele in Lanai City, ☎ 800/
321-4666, greens fees $225 or $190
for guests), a traditional par-72
course, designed by Greg Norman
with very different front and back 9
holes. If you have time, have dinner
in Lanai City at **⑧D Hulopoe Court**
(p 160) in the Lodge at Koele. I recommend the grilled Hawaiian opakapaka with an Asian green salad with
mango sauce. If you have kids, you
could try the Hulopo'e pizza with a
choice of pineapple, prosciutto, red
peppers, olives, and mushrooms.

Munro Trail.

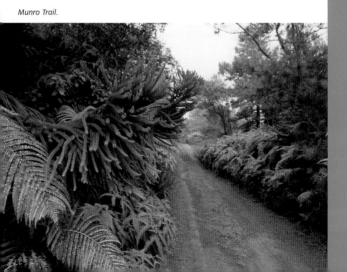

Where to Stay & Dine

★★★ kids Four Seasons Resort at Manele Bay

HULOPOE BAY This hotel steps down the hillside to one of Hawaii's best stretches of golden sand. Most of the spacious airy rooms open to breath-taking views. *Hulopoe Beach.* ☎ *800/321-4666; www.fourseasons. com/lanai. 236 units. $395–$925 double. AE, DC, MC, V. Map p 156.*

★ kids Hotel Lanai LANAI CITY

This hotel is perfect for families and other vacationers who are looking for a good deal. Built in the 1920s, it's a clapboard plantation-era relic that has retained its quaint character. *828 Lanai Ave., Lanai City.* ☎ *800/795-7211; www.hotellanai. com. 11 units. $115–$135 double; $175 cottage double. Rates include continental breakfast. AE, MC, V. Map p 156.*

★ The Lodge at Koele LANAI

CITY This lodge resembles a grand English country estate and is in the cool mist of the mountains, 8 miles (12.9km) inland from any beach. In the winter, temperatures can drop into the 50s. *Lanai City.* ☎ *800/321-4666; www.fourseasons.com/lanai. 102 units. $350–$475 double. AE, DC, MC, V. Map p 156.*

Blue Ginger Café LANAI CITY

COFFEE SHOP This is a casual, inexpensive alternative to Lanai's fancy hotel restaurants. Try the popular hamburgers on homemade buns. *409 Seventh St. (at Ilima St.), Lanai City.* ☎ *808/565-6363. Breakfast and lunch items under $7.50; dinner under $15. No credit cards. Breakfast, lunch & dinner daily. Map p 156.*

★★ kids Henry Clay's Rotisserie LANAI CITY *CAJUN/COUNTRY

CUISINE* Henry Clay Richardson, a New Orleans native, has brought Cajun and regional cuisine to Lanai. In the Hotel Lanai. *828 Lanai Ave., Lanai City.* ☎ *808/565-7211; www. hotellanai.com. Main courses $19– $33. MC, V. Dinner daily. Map p 156.*

★★★ Ihilani HULOPOE BAY *ITAL-

IAN* Overlooking the resort and the ocean beyond, this classy dining room serves a range of well prepared dishes that includes an inspired lobster risotto. *Four Seasons–Lanai at Manele Bay.* ☎ *808/565-2296. Main courses $21–$44. AE, DC, MC, V. Dinner Tues–Sat. Map p 156.*

★★ Pele's Other Garden LANAI

CITY *DELI/BISTRO* Excellent pizza, sandwiches, fresh organic produce, fresh juices, and special items such as top-quality black-bean burritos, roasted red peppers, and stuffed grape leaves make this place a Lanai City must. *811 Houston St., Lanai City.* ☎ *808/565-9628. Most lunch items less than $8; pizza from $7; dinner items $17–$20. AE, DISC, MC, V. Brunch & dinner Mon–Fri; dinner Sat. Map p 156.*

★ Ocean Grill HULOPOE BAY

SEAFOOD The Ocean Grill serves an interesting variety of wraps, sandwiches, salads, and entrees at lunch. The alfresco dinner, during which you can watch first the sunset, then the stars, features fresh local fish, beef, pork chops, rack of lamb, and chicken. *Four Seasons– Lanai at Manele Bay.* ☎ *808/565- 2092. Lunch $15–$18; dinner $30–$44. AE, DC, MC, V. Daily lunch; Thurs–Mon dinner. Map p 156.* ●

The
Savvy Traveler

Before You Go

Government Tourist Offices

On Maui: Maui Visitors Bureau, 1727 Wili Pa Loop, Wailuku, HI 96793. ☎ 800/525-MAUI; www. visitmaui.com. **On Lanai:** Lanai Visitors Bureau, P.O. Box 631436, Lanai City, HI 96763. ☎ 800/947-4774; www.visitlanai.net.

The Best Times to Go

Most visitors don't come to Maui when the weather's best in the islands; rather, they come when it's at its worst everywhere else. Thus, the **high season**—when prices are up and resorts are booked to capacity—generally runs from mid-December through March or mid-April. The last 2 weeks of December in particular are the prime time for travel to Maui. If you're planning a holiday trip, make your reservations as early as possible, count on holiday crowds, and expect to pay top dollar for accommodations, car rentals, and airfare. Whale-watching season begins in December and continues through the rest of winter, sometimes lasting into May.

The **off seasons,** when the best rates are available, spring (mid-Apr–mid-June) and fall (Sept–mid-Dec), are also Maui's best seasons in terms of reliably great weather. If you're looking to save money, or if you just want to avoid the crowds, this is the time to visit. Hotel rates and airfares tend to be significantly lower and good package deals are often available.

Note: If you plan to come to Maui between the last week in April and the first week in May, be sure to book your accommodations, interisland air reservations, and car rental in advance. In Japan, the last week of April is called **Golden Week,** because three Japanese holidays

take place one after the other. The islands are especially busy with Japanese tourists during this time.

Due to the large number of families traveling in **summer** (June–Aug), you won't get the fantastic bargains of spring and fall. However, you'll still do much better on packages, airfare, and accommodations than you will in winter.

Festivals & Special Events

WINTER. The **Lighting of the Banyan Tree,** Lahaina's historic Banyan Tree is lit up with thousands of Christmas lights in early December (☎ 888/310-1117; www.visit lahaina.com). The end of December and early January brings the Academy of Motion Pictures' major screenings of top films with the **First Light,** at the Maui Arts and Cultural Center (☎ 808/579-9996; www.mauifilmfestival.com). To celebrate **Chinese New Year** (Jan–Feb), the historic Wo Hing Temple in Lahaina town holds a traditional lion dance plus fireworks, food booths, and a host of activities (☎ 888/310-1117; www.visitlanai.net). **Whale Day Celebration,** February, is a day-long celebration in Kalama Park in Kihei, with a parade, entertainment, a crafts fair, games, and food (☎ 808/249-8811; www.visitmaui. com).

SPRING. In mid-March, the entire town of Lahaina celebrates **Ocean Arts Festival,** in Banyan Tree Park, with Hawaiian musicians and hula troupes, marine-related activities, games, and a "creature feature" touch-pool exhibit for children (☎ 888/310-1117; www.visitlahaina. com). At the end of March or early April, Hana holds the **East Maui Taro Festival,** serving taro in many different forms, from poi to chips.

Also on hand are Hawaiian exhibits, demonstrations, and food booths (☎ 808/248-8972; www.calendar maui.com). Easter weekend brings the **Annual Ritz-Carlton Kapalua Celebration of the Arts** with Maui artists providing free hands-on lessons (☎ 808/669-6200; www. celebrationofthearts.org). May 1 is the **Annual Lei Day Celebration** throughout the island, with lei-making contests, pageantry, arts and crafts, and concerts (☎ 808/875-4100; www.visitmaui.com).

SUMMER. A state holiday on June 10, **King Kamehameha Day,** jumpstarts the summer with a massive floral parade and *hoolaulea* (party) (☎ 888/310-1117; www.visitlahaina. com). Just before Father's Day weekend in June, the **Maui Film Festival** at the Wailea Resort features 5 days and nights of premieres and special films, along with traditional Hawaiian storytelling, chants, hula, and contemporary music (☎ 808/579-9996; mauifilmfestival.com). In late June, the **Hawaiian Slack-Key Guitar Festival** at the Maui Arts and Cultural Center brings great performances by the best musicians in Hawaii (☎ 808/239-4336; www. hawaiianslackkeyguitarfestivals. com). On the first Saturday in July, on Lanai, the **Pineapple Festival** celebrates Lanai's history of pineapple

plantation and ranching and includes pineapple-eating and -cooking contests, entertainment, arts and crafts, food, and fireworks (☎ 808/565-7600; www.visitlanai.net). The **Fourth of July** is celebrated on Maui with various activities (☎ 800/525-MAUI; www.visitmaui.com). Throughout June and July, various Buddhist churches celebrate **Bon Dance and Lantern Ceremony,** a colorful ceremony honoring the souls of the dead (☎ 808/661-4304; www.visitmaui.com). In early July, famous wine and food experts and oenophiles gather at the **Kapalua Wine and Food Festival** (☎ 800/KAPALUA; www.kapaluaresort.com), for tastings, panel discussions, and samplings of new releases. In early August, the **Maui Onion Festival** takes place in Whalers Village, Kaanapali, featuring everything you ever wanted to know about the sweetest onions in the world, plus the Maui Onion Cook-Off (☎ 808/661-4567; www.whalersvillage.com).

FALL. The statewide **Aloha Festivals** (☎ 800/852-7690; www.aloha festivals.com), a series of celebrations, parades, and other events honoring the Hawaiian culture, takes place in September and October. Early September brings the **LifeFest Kapalua** (☎ 866/669-2440; www .lifefestmaui.com) at the Kapalua

Keeping Costs Down

- Travel during Maui's "off-season" of Mid-April to mid-June and again from September to December. Accommodations, car rentals and air fares are much cheaper.
- Try to get a package deal of air-car-accommodations, which can save you a bundle.
- Stay in a condominium, which has kitchen facilities, saving you to have to eat out for every meal.
- Make picnic lunches and sunset dinners with inexpensive takeout meals or cook your own in your condo kitchen.

LAHAINA-KAANAPALI'S AVERAGE TEMPERATURE & RAINFALL

	JAN	FEB	MAR	APR	MAY	JUNE
Daily High (°F)	82	80	83	84	85	87
Daily Low (°F)	64	63	64	65	67	68
Water temp	75	74	74	75	76	77
Rain in inches	3.5	2.4	1.8	1.1	1.1	0.1

	JULY	AUG	SEPT	OCT	NOV	DEC
Daily High (°F)	88	88	89	88	86	83
Daily Low (°F)	69	69	70	69	67	65
Water temp	78	79	80	79	77	76
Rain in inches	0.2	0.2	0.3	1.1	2.2	3.2

KIHEI-WAILEA'S AVERAGE TEMPERATURE & RAINFALL

	JAN	FEB	MAR	APR	MAY	JUNE
Daily High (°F)	81	81	83	84	85	87
Daily Low (°F)	63	63	64	64	65	67
Water temp	75	74	74	75	76	77
Days of Precip.	2.5	1.6	1.0	0.7	0.5	0.4

	JULY	AUG	SEPT	OCT	NOV	DEC
Daily High (°F)	88	89	88	87	85	82
Daily Low (°F)	69	69	69	68	67	65
Water temp	78	79	80	79	77	76
Days of Precip.	0.5	0.3	0.7	1.3	1.7	2.3

Resort, a 3-day health-and-wellness event featuring lectures and panel presentations by leaders in the health and wellness field, plus ocean sporting events, fitness activities, a health and wellness expo, and sumptuous gala dinners. Also in early September is **A Taste of Lahaina,** where Maui's premier chefs serve up 40 signature entrees. Includes cooking demonstrations, wine tastings, and live entertainment (☎ *888/310-1117; www.visit lahaina.com*). **Halloween in Lahaina** is a giant costume party (some 30,000 people show up) on the streets of Lahaina (☎ *888/310-1117; www.visitlahaina.com*).

The Weather

Because Maui lies at the edge of the tropical zone, it technically has only two seasons, both of them warm. The dry season corresponds to summer, and the rainy season generally runs from November to March. The rainy season can cause gray weather and spoil your tanning opportunities. Fortunately, it seldom rains for more than 3 days straight, and rainy days often just consist of a mix of clouds and sun, with very brief showers.

The **year-round temperature** usually varies no more than 15°F (9°C), but it depends on where you are. Maui's **leeward** sides (the west and south) are usually hot and dry, whereas the **windward** sides (east and north) are generally cooler and moist. If you want arid, desertlike weather, go leeward. If you want lush, often wet, junglelike weather, go windward. Your best bets for total year-round sun are the Kihei-Wailea and Lahaina-Kapalua coasts.

Maui is also full of **microclimates,** thanks to its interior valleys, coastal plains, and mountain peaks. If you travel into the mountains, it can change from summer to winter in a matter of hours, because it's cooler the higher up you go.

Useful Websites

- **www.visitmaui.com:** All-around guide to Maui and Lanai.

- **www.hawaiiradiotv.com/puka. html:** Links to some 200-plus websites in Hawaii.

- **www.planet-hawaii.com:** An island guide to activities, lodging, shopping, culture, the surf report, weather, and more.

- **www.islandcurrents.com:** Specializes in arts and culture.

- **www.maui.net:** Directory of links to accommodations, activities, and shopping.

- **www.geocities.com/~olelo:** Hawaiian language website with easy lessons on Hawaiian and a cultural calendar.

- **www.visitlanai.net:** Information on the island of Lanai.

- **www.weather.com**: Up-to-the-minute worldwide weather reports.

Restaurant & Activity Reservations

Book well in advance if you're determined to eat at a particular spot or participate in a certain activity (like the Trilogy sailing-snorkeling trip to Lanai or scuba diving around Molokini). For popular restaurants, if you didn't call in advance, try asking for early or late hours—often tables are available before 6:30pm and after 9pm. You could also call the day before or first thing in the morning, when you may be able to take advantage of a cancellation.

Cell (Mobile) Phones

In general it's a good bet that your phone will work in Maui, although coverage may not be as good as in your hometown. Cell coverage on Lanai may be spotty (few towers). If you're not from the U.S., you'll be appalled at the poor reach of the GSM (Global System for Mobiles) wireless network, which is used by much of the rest of the world. (To see where GSM phones work in the U.S., check out www.t-mobile.com/coverage/national_popup.asp). And you may or may not be able to send SMS (text messages) overseas. Assume nothing—call your wireless provider and get the full scoop. In a worst-case scenario, you can always rent a phone from InTouch USA (☎ 800/872-7626; www.intouchglobal.com), but be aware that you'll pay $1 a minute or more for airtime.

Getting **There**

By Plane

If possible, fly directly to Maui. Doing so can save you a 2-hour layover in Honolulu and another plane ride. If you're headed for Lanai, you'll have to connect through Honolulu.

If you think of the island of Maui as the shape of a person's head and shoulders, you'll probably arrive on its neck, at **Kahului Airport.**

At press time, 12 airlines (and 1 code-share airline) flew directly from the U.S. mainland and Canada to Kahului (see "Toll-free Numbers & Websites on p 176 for contact information): **Aloha Airlines** has nonstop service from Oakland, Orange County, Reno, and San Diego; **American Airlines** flies direct from Dallas–Fort Worth, Chicago, and Los Angeles; **American West** has nonstop service from Phoenix and Las Vegas; **Continental** has flights from Los Angeles; **Delta Airlines** offers direct flights from Salt Lake City and Los Angeles; **Hawaiian Airlines** has direct flights from Portland and Seattle; **Northwest Airlines** has a direct flight from Seattle; **Southwest Airlines** has flights from Oakland, Los Angeles, and Phoenix via **American Trans Air; Delta** has nonstop flights from Salt Lake City and Los Angeles; and **United Airlines** offers daily

nonstop flights from San Francisco, Los Angeles, and Chicago. Carriers flying from Vancouver to Maui include: **Air Canada; Harmony Airways,** which also has a direct flight from Calgary; and **West Jet.**

Other carriers fly to Honolulu, where you'll have to pick up an inter-island flight to Maui. (The airlines listed in the paragraph above also offer many more flights to Honolulu from additional cities on the mainland.) Both **Aloha Airlines** and **Hawaiian Airlines** offer jet service from Honolulu to Maui. Mesa Air Group recently began interisland flights from Honolulu to Maui on **go!**

Getting **Around**

By Car

The only way to get around Maui is to rent a car. There is no real public transportation on Maui. The best way to get a good deal on a car rental is to book online. Maui's car-rental rates run about $47 a day (including all state taxes and fees). Cars are usually plentiful, except on holiday weekends, which in Hawaii also means King Kamehameha Day (June 11), Prince Kuhio Day (Mar 26), and Admission Day (3rd Fri in Aug). Rental cars are usually at a premium on Lanai, so book well ahead.

All the major car-rental agencies have offices on Maui: **Alamo** (☎ 800/327-9633; www.goalamo.com), **Avis** (☎ 800/321-3712; www.avis.com), **Budget** (☎ 800/572-0700; www.budget.com), **Dollar** (☎ 800/800-4000; www.dollarcar.com), **Hertz** (☎ 800/654-3011; www.hertz.com), and **National** (☎ 800/227-7368; www.nationalcar.com).

There are also a few frugal car-rental agencies offering older cars

at discount prices. **Word of Mouth Rent-a-Used-Car** (☎ 800/533-5929 or 808/877-2436; www.mauirentacar.com) has Toyota and Nissans from 1995 to 2004 that start at $27 a day (air-conditioned, four door), including all taxes, with a 3-day minimum, or from $156 a week. Free airport pickup and drop-off included. **Maui Cruisers,** in Wailuku (☎ 877/749-7889 or 808/249-2319; www.mauicruisers.net), also offers free airport pickup and return on their 8-to10- year-old Nissan Sentras and Toyota Corrollas; rentals start at $31 a day (3-day minimum) or $175 a week (including tax and insurance).

To rent a car in Hawaii, you must be at least 25 years old and have a valid driver's license and a credit card.

One more thing on car rentals: Hawaii is a no-fault state, which means that if you don't have collision-damage insurance, you are required to pay for all damages before you leave the state, whether or not the accident was your fault. Your personal car insurance back home may provide rental-car coverage; read your policy or call your insurer before you leave home. Bring your insurance identification card if you decline the optional insurance, which usually costs from $12 to $20 a day. Obtain the name of your company's local claim representative before you go. Some credit card companies also provide collision-damage insurance for their customers; check with yours before you rent.

By Taxi

You'll see taxis outside the airport terminal, but note that they are quite expensive—expect to spend around $60 to $75 for a ride from Kahului to Kaanapali and $50 from the airport to Wailea. For island-wide 24-hour service, call **Alii Cab Co.** (☎ 808/661-3688 or 808/667-2605). You can also try **Kihei Taxi** (☎ 808/879-3000), **Wailea Taxi** (☎ 808/874-5000), or **Maui Central Cab** (☎ 808/244-7278).

Fast **Facts**

ATMS   Hawaii pioneered the use of **ATMs** nearly 3 decades ago, and now they're everywhere. You'll find them at most banks, in supermarkets, and in most resorts and shopping centers. **Cirrus** (☎ 800/424-7787; www.mastercard.com) and **PLUS** (☎ 800/843-7587; www.visa.com) are the two most popular networks; check the back of your ATM card to see which network your bank belongs to (most banks belong to both these days).

BABYSITTING   The first place to check is with your hotel. Many hotels have babysitting services or will provide you with lists of reliable sitters. You can also call **People Attentive to Children** (PATCH; ☎ 808/242-9232; www.patch hawaii.org), which will refer you to individuals who have taken their training courses on child care. If you are traveling to Lanai, call ☎ 800/498-4145.

BANKING HOURS   Bank hours are Monday through Thursday from 8:30am to 3pm, Friday from 8:30am to 6pm; some banks are open on Saturday.

B&BS   The top reservations service for bed and breakfasts is **Hawaii's**

Best Bed & Breakfasts (☎ 800/262-9912; www.bestbnb.com).

BUSINESS HOURS   Most offices are open from 8am to 5pm. Shopping centers are open Monday through Friday from 10am to 9pm, Saturday from 10am to 5:30pm, and Sunday from 10am to 5 or 6pm.

CLIMATE   See "The Weather" on p 164.

CONCERTS   See chapter 10, p 143.

CONDOMINIUM & VACATION HOME RENTALS   For condos, I recommend **Bello Realty** (☎ 800/541-3060; www.bellomauivacations.com); for vacation rentals, contact **Hawaiian Beach Rentals** (☎ 808/262-69368; www.hawaiianbeachrentals.com) or **Hawaii Condo Exchange** (☎ 800/442-0404; http://hawaiicondo exchange.com).

CONSULATES & EMBASSIES   All embassies are located in Washington, D.C. If your country isn't listed, call for directory information in Washington, D.C. (☎ 202/555-1212), for the number of your national embassy. The embassy of **Australia** is at 1601 Massachusetts Ave. NW, Washington, DC 20036 (☎ 202/797-3000; www.austemb.org). The embassy of **Canada** is at

501 Pennsylvania Ave. NW, Washington, DC 20001 (☎ 202/682-1740; www.canadianembassy.org). The embassy of **Ireland** is at 2234 Massachusetts Ave. NW, Washington, DC 20008 (☎ 202/462-3939; www.irelandemb.org). The embassy of the **United Kingdom** is at 3100 Massachusetts Ave. NW, Washington, DC 20008 (☎ 202/588-7800; www.britainusa.com/consular/embassy).

CREDIT CARDS Credit cards are a safe way to "carry" money, they provide a convenient record of all your expenses, and they generally offer good exchange rates. You can also withdraw cash advances from your credit cards at banks or ATMs, provided you know your PIN.

CUSTOMS Visitors arriving by air, no matter what the port of entry, should cultivate patience and resignation before setting foot on U.S. soil. Getting through customs and immigration control can take as long as 2 hours on some days. Travelers arriving from Canada will clear immigration and customs at their city of departure, which is much quicker.

DENTISTS If you have dental problems, a nationwide referral service known as 1-800-DENTIST (☎ 800/336-8478) will provide the name of a nearby dentist or clinic. Emergency dental care is available at **Kihei Dental Center,** 1847 S. Kihei Rd., Kihei (☎ 808/874-8401), or in Lahaina at the **Aloha Lahaina Dentists,** 134 Luakini St. (in the Maui Medical Group Building) (☎ 808/661-4005).

DINING With a few exceptions at the high-end of the scale, dining attire is fairly casual. It's a good idea to make reservations in advance if you plan on eating between 7 and 9pm.

DOCTORS No appointment is necessary at **West Maui Healthcare Center,** Whalers Village, 2435 Kaanapali Pkwy., Suite H-7 (near Leilani's Restaurant), Kaanapali

(☎ 808/667-9721), which is open 365 days a year until 10pm. In Kihei call **Urgent Care,** 1325 S. Kihei Rd., Suite 103 (at Lipoa St., across from Star Market; ☎ 808/879-7781), open daily from 6am to midnight; doctors are on call 24 hours a day.

ELECTRICITY Like Canada, the United States uses 110 to 120 volts AC (60 cycles), compared to 220 to 240 volts AC (50 cycles) in most of Europe, Australia, and New Zealand. If your small appliances use 220 to 240 volts, you'll need a 110-volt transformer and a plug adapter with two flat parallel pins to operate them. Downward converters that change 220–240 volts to 110–120 volts are difficult to find in the United States, so bring one with you.

EMERGENCIES Dial ☎ 911 for the police, an ambulance, and the fire department. District stations are located in Lahaina (☎ 808/661-4441) and in Hana (☎ 808/248-8311). For the **Poison Control Center,** call ☎ 800/362-3585.

EVENT LISTINGS The best source for listings is the Friday edition of the local daily newspaper, *Maui News* (www.mauinews.com). There are also several tourist publications with listings: *This Week on Maui* (www.thisweek.com) and *Maui Visitor Magazine* (www.visitormagazines.com). You can also check small, local community newspapers: *Maui Times* (www.mauitime.com); *Maui Weekly* (www.mauiweekly.com); *Lahaina News* (www.lahainanews.com); and the *Haleakala Times* (www.haleakalatimes.com).

FAMILY TRAVEL You might want to purchase a copy of *Frommer's Hawaii with Kids,* a guidebook dedicated to family visits to Hawaii. For family-friendly events, check out the Friday edition of the *Maui News,* the daily island newspaper, for events.

GAY & LESBIAN TRAVELERS The **International Gay & Lesbian Travel Association (IGLTA)**

(☎ 800/448-8550 or 954/776-2626; www.iglta.org) is the trade association for the gay and lesbian travel industry, and offers an online directory of gay- and lesbian-friendly travel businesses. For information on gay-friendly business, accommodations, and gay-owned and gay-friendly lodgings: **Pacific Ocean Holidays,** P.O. Box 88245, Honolulu, HI 96830 (☎ 800/735-6600; www.gayhawaii.com).

HOLIDAYS   Federal, state, and county government offices are closed on all federal holidays: January 1 (New Year's Day); third Monday in January (Martin Luther King, Jr. Day); third Monday in February (Presidents' Day, Washington's Birthday); last Monday in May (Memorial Day); July 4th (Independence Day); first Monday in September (Labor Day); second Monday in October (Columbus Day); November 11 (Veterans' Day); fourth Thursday in November (Thanksgiving Day); and December 25 (Christmas). State and county offices also are closed on local holidays, including Prince Kuhio Day (Mar 26); King Kamehameha Day (June 11); and Admission Day (third Fri in Aug). Other special days celebrated by many people in Hawaii but that do not involve the closing of federal, state, or county offices are: Chinese New Year (in Jan or Feb), Girls' Day (Mar 3), Buddha's Birthday (Apr 8), Father Damien's Day (Apr 15), Boys' Day (May 5), Samoan Flag Day (in Aug), Aloha Festivals (Sept or Oct), and Pearl Harbor Day (Dec 7).

INSURANCE   Trip-cancellation insurance helps you get your money back if you have to back out of a trip, if you have to go home early, or if your travel supplier goes bankrupt. Allowed reasons for cancellation can range from sickness to natural disasters to the State Department declaring your destination unsafe for travel. In this unstable world, trip-cancellation insurance is a good buy if you're getting tickets well in advance. Insurance policy details vary, so read the fine print—and especially make sure that your airline or cruise line is on the list of carriers covered in case of bankruptcy. For information, contact one of the following insurers: **Access America** (☎ 866/807-3982; www.accessamerica.com); **Travel Guard International** (☎ 800/826-4919; www.travelguard.com); **Travel Insured International** (☎ 800/243-3174; www.travelinsured.com); and **Travelex Insurance Services** (☎ 888/457-4602; www.travelex-insurance.com).

Although it's not required of travelers, health insurance is highly recommended. Unlike many European countries, the United States does not usually offer free or low-cost medical care to its citizens or visitors. Doctors and hospitals are expensive, and in most cases will require advance payment or proof of coverage before they render their services. Though lack of health insurance may prevent you from being admitted to a hospital in non-emergencies, don't worry about being left on a street corner to die: The American way is to fix you now and bill the living daylights out of you later.

Insurance for British Travelers: Most big travel agents offer their own insurance and will probably try to sell you their package when you book a holiday. Think before you sign. Britain's Consumers' Association recommends that you insist on seeing the policy and reading the fine print before buying travel insurance. The **Association of British Insurers** (☎ 020/7600-3333; www.abi.org.uk) gives advice by phone and publishes *Holiday Insurance,* a free guide to policy provisions and prices. You might also shop around for better deals: Try **Columbus Direct** (☎ 020/7375-0011; www.columbusdirect.net).

Insurance for Canadian Travelers: Canadians should check with their provincial health plan offices or call Health Canada (☎ 613/957-2991; www.hc-sc.gc.ca) to find out the extent of your coverage and what documentation and receipts you must take home in case you are treated in the United States.

Lost-Luggage Insurance: On domestic flights, checked baggage is covered *up to* $2,800 per ticketed passenger. Note the key words "up to," which does not mean you collect $2,800 if they lose your bag. When you read the fine print on your ticket you often wonder what the heck they do cover as they explicitly state they have **NO** liability for damage or loss of protruding baggage parts (wheels, straps, pockets, pull handles, and so on), and **NO** liability for photographic equipment, computers, VCRs, and any other electronic equipment including software or components, jewelry, cash, documents, furs, works of art, or other similar valuable items. On international flights (including U.S. portions of international trips), baggage liability is limited to $9.07 per pound ($20 per kg) or a maximum of 70 lbs/32 kgs ($634.90) per checked bag. If you plan to check items more valuable than the standard liability, see if your valuables are covered by your homeowner's policy or get baggage insurance as part of your comprehensive travel-insurance package. Don't buy insurance at the airport, as it's usually overpriced. Be sure to take any valuables or irreplaceable items with you in your carry-on luggage. If your luggage is lost, immediately file a lost-luggage claim at the airport, detailing the luggage contents (always carry a list in your carry on). For most airlines, you must report delayed, damaged, or lost baggage within 4 hours of arrival. The airlines are required to deliver luggage, once found, directly to your house or destination free of charge.

INTERNET ACCESS Major hotels and even small B&Bs have Internet access; many of them have also have Wi-Fi. Just check the charges ahead of time, they can be exorbitant. The best Internet deal on Maui is the **public libraries** (to find the closest location, check www.publiclibraries.com/hawaii.htm), which offer free access if you have a library card; a 3-month visitor card costs $10. In Kihei you can go to the **Hale Imua Internet Café,** in the Kamaole Center (☎ 808/891-9219). In Lahaina drop by **Buns of Maui,** Old Lahaina Shopping Center, 878 Front St. (☎ 808/661-5407), which has the cheapest rates on Maui at only 8 cents a minute and no minimum.

MAIL & POSTAGE To find the nearest post office, call ☎ 800/ASK-USPS or log on to www.usps.gov. In Lahaina the main post office is at the Lahaina Civic Center, 1760 Honoapiilani Hwy.; in Kahului there's a branch at 138 S. Puunene Ave.; and in Kihei there's one at 1254 S. Kihei Rd. Mail can be sent to you, in your name, c/o General Delivery, at the post office. Most post offices will hold your mail for up to 1 month. At press time, domestic postage rates were 24¢ for a postcard and 39¢ for a letter. For international mail, a first-class letter of up to 1 ounce costs 63¢ and a first-class postcard costs 55¢.

MONEY Don't carry a lot of cash in your wallet. Many small restaurants won't accept credit cards, so ask upfront if you plan to pay with plastic. Traveler's checks are something of an anachronism from the days before ATMs; **American Express** (☎ 800/221-7282), **Visa** (☎ 800/732-1322), and **MasterCard** (☎ 800/223-9920) all offer them. If you choose to carry traveler's checks, be sure to keep a record of their serial numbers separate from your checks in the event that they are stolen or lost.

PASSPORTS Always keep a photocopy of your passport with you (but separate from your passport) when you're traveling. If your passport is lost or stolen, having a copy significantly facilitates the reissuing process at your consulate. Keep your passport and other valuables in your room's safe or in the hotel safe.

PHARMACIES There are no 24-hour pharmacies on Maui. I recommend Longs Drug Stores (www.longs.com), which has two pharmacies: 1215 South Kihei Rd. Kihei (☎ 808/879-2033), and in the Maui Mall Shopping Center, 70 E. Kaahumanu Ave., Kahului (☎ 808/877-0068).

SAFETY Although Hawaii is generally a safe tourist destination, visitors have been crime victims, so stay alert. The most common crime against tourists is rental-car break-ins. Never leave any valuables in your car, not even in your trunk. Be especially careful at high-risk areas such as beaches and resorts. Never carry large amounts of cash with you. Stay in well-lighted areas after dark. Don't hike on deserted trails or swim in the ocean alone.

SENIOR TRAVELERS Discounts for seniors are available at almost all of Maui's major attractions, and occasionally at hotels and restaurants. Always inquire when making hotel reservations, and especially when you're buying your airline ticket—most major domestic airlines offer senior discounts. Members of **AARP** (☎ 800/424-3410 or 202/434-2277; www.aarp.org) are usually eligible for such discounts. AARP also puts together organized tour packages at moderate rates. Some great, low-cost trips to Hawaii are offered to people 55 and older through **Elderhostel,** 75 Federal St., Boston, MA 02110 (☎ 617/426-8056; www.elderhostel.org), a nonprofit group that arranges travel and study programs around the world. You can obtain a complete catalog of offerings by writing to Elderhostel, P.O. Box 1959, Wakefield, MA 01880-5959. If you're planning to visit Haleakala National Park, you can save sightseeing dollars if you're 62 or older by picking up a **Golden Age Passport** from any national park, recreation area, or monument. This lifetime pass has a one-time fee of \$10 and provides free admission to all of the parks in the system, plus a 50% savings on camping and recreation fees. Be sure to have proof of your age with you.

SPECTATOR SPORTS You've got your choice of **golf tournaments** (☎ 808/669-2440; visit www.kapaluamaui.com); **polo** (☎ 808/877-7744 and 808/572-7326; www.visitmaui.com); **Hawaiian outrigger canoe races,** from May to September (☎ 808/261-6615; www.y2kanu.com); **wind surfing** (☎ 808/877-2111; www.vrmaui.com/maui/hookipa.htm); and **rodeo** (☎ 808/572-9565; www.visitmaui.com).

TAXES Hawaii's sales tax is 4%. Hotel occupancy tax is 7.25%, and the state allows hoteliers to tack on an additional .001666% excise tax. Thus, expect taxes of about 11.42% to be added to every hotel bill.

TAXIS See "Getting Around," above.

TELEPHONE For directory assistance, dial ☎ 411; for long-distance information, dial 1, then the appropriate area code and 555-1212. Pay phones cost 50¢ for local calls (all calls on the island of Maui are local calls). The area code for all of Hawaii (not just Maui) is 808. Calls to other islands are considered long distance. All calls made to another island you have to dial 1 + 808 + the 7 digit phone number.

TIPPING Tipping is ingrained in the American way of life. Here are some rules of thumb: In hotels, tip bellhops at least \$1 per bag (\$2–\$3 if you have a lot of luggage), and tip the chamber staff \$1 to \$2 per person per day (more if you've left a disaster area for him or her to clean up, or if you're traveling with kids and/or pets). Tip the doorman or concierge only if he or she has provided you with some specific service (like calling a cab). In restaurants, bars, and nightclubs, tip service staff 15% to 20% of the check, and tip bartenders 10% to 15%. Tipping is not expected in cafeterias and fast-food restaurants. Tip cab drivers 15% of the fare and tip skycaps at airports at least $1 per bag ($2–$3 if you have a lot of luggage).

TOILETS   Your best bet is Starbucks or a fast food restaurant. You can also head to hotel lobbies and shopping centers. Parks have restrooms, but generally they are not very clean and may be in need of major repairs.

TOURIST OFFICE   See Government Tourist Offices on p 162.

TRAVELERS WITH DISABILITIES   Travelers with disabilities are made to feel very welcome in Maui. Hotels are usually equipped with wheelchair-accessible rooms, and tour companies provide many special services. Contact the **Center for Independent Living Maui,** 220 Imi Kala Street, Suite 103, Wailuku, HI 96793 (☎ 808/242-4966; TTY: 808/242-4968; mcilogg@gte.net; no

website). The only travel agency in Hawaii specializing in needs for travelers with disabilities is **Access Aloha Travel** (☎ 800/480-1143; www.accessalohatravel.com), which can book anything, including rental vans, accommodations, tours, cruises, airfare, and just about anything else you can think of. Travelers with disabilities who wish to do their own driving can rent hand-controlled cars from **Avis** (☎ 800/331-1212; www.avis.com) and **Hertz** (☎ 800/654-3131; www.hertz.com). The number of hand-controlled cars in Hawaii is limited, so be sure to book well in advance. For wheelchair-accessible vans, contact **Accessible Vans of Hawaii,** 186 Mehani Circle, Kihei (☎ 800/303-3750; www.accessiblevans.com). Maui recognizes other states' windshield placards indicating that the driver of the car is disabled, so be sure to bring yours with you. Vision-impaired travelers who use a Seeing-Eye dog need to present documentation that the dog is a trained Seeing-Eye dog and has had rabies shots. For more information, contact the Animal Quarantine Facility (☎ 808/483-7171; www.hawaii.gov).

A Brief **History**

AROUND A.D. 700 Paddling outrigger canoes, the first ancestors of today's Hawaiians follow the stars and birds across the sea to Hawaii.

AROUND 1300 Transoceanic voyages halt; Hawaii begins to develop its own culture in earnest. The settlers build temples, fishponds, and aqueducts to irrigate taro plantations. Sailors become farmers and fishermen. Each island is

a separate kingdom. The *alii* (chiefs) create a caste system and establish taboos. Violators are strangled. High priests ask the gods Lono and Ku for divine guidance. Ritual human sacrifices are common.

AROUND 1500 Piilani, from Hana, unites Maui, builds fishponds and irrigation fields, and begins creating a paved road some 4- to 6-feet (1.2–1.8km) wide around the entire island. Piilani's sons and his grandson complete the project.

1759 Kalaniopuu, a chief from the Big Island, captures Hana from the powerful Maui chief Kahikili, while Kahikili is busy overtaking Molokai. The Molokai chief escapes and flees with his wife to Hana, where the Big Island chief welcomes him. A few years later, the Molokai chief and his wife have a baby girl in Hana, named Kaahumanu, who later marries Kamehameha. During her lifetime she makes major changes in Hawaii's culture, breaking the taboo against women eating with men and converting to Christianity. The latter leads the way for thousands of Hawaiians to adopt the religion of their queen.

1778 Captain James Cook sails into Waimea Bay on Kauai, where he is welcomed as the god Lono. Overnight, Stone Age Hawaii enters the age of iron. Nails are traded for freshwater, pigs, and the affections of Hawaiian women. The sailors bring syphilis, measles, and other diseases to which the Hawaiians have no natural immunity, thereby unwittingly wreaking havoc on the native population.

FEBRUARY 14, 1779 Cook and four of his crew are killed in Kealakekua Bay on the Big Island.

1782 Kamehameha I begins his campaign to unify the Hawaiian islands.

1790 Using western weapons (guns and canons), Kamehameha successfully defeats (and slays) the warriors of Maui's chief Kahekili at Iao. After conquering Maui 5 years later, Kamehameha makes Lahaina the capitol of his new united kingdom, stopping there in 1801 with his fleet of Pelehu war canoes on his way to do battle on Oahu and Kauai. Kame-

hameha stays in Lahaina for a year, constructing the "Brick Palace," Hawaii's first Western-style structure.

1810 Kamehameha I unites the Hawaiian Islands.

1819 Kamehameha I dies, his son Liholiho is proclaimed Kamehameha II; under the influence of Queen Kaahumanu, Kamehameha II orders the destruction of *heiau* and an end to the *kapu* system, thus overthrowing the traditional Hawaiian religion. The first whaling ship, *Bellina*, drops anchor in Lahaina.

1823 Missionaries arrive in Lahaina from New England, bent on converting the pagans. The missionaries clothe the natives, ban them from dancing the hula, and nearly dismantle their ancient culture. They try to keep the whalers and sailors out of the bawdy houses, where whiskey flows freely and the virtue of native women is never safe.

1845 King Kamehameha III moves the capital of Hawaii from Lahaina to Honolulu, whose natural harbor can accommodate more commerce.

1849 George Wilfong, a cantankerous sea captain, builds a mill in Hana and plants some 60 acres of sugar cane, creating Hawaii's first sugar plantation.

1876 An elaborate ditch system that takes water from rainy Haiku to the dry plains of Wailuku some 17 miles (27.4km) away, cements the future of sugar in Maui.

JANUARY 17, 1893 A group of American sugar planters and missionary descendants, with the support of U.S. Marines, imprison Queen Liliuokalani in her own palace in Honolulu and illegally overthrow the Hawaiian government.

DECEMBER 7, 1941 Japanese Zeros bomb American warships based at Pearl Harbor, plunging the United States into World War II.

MARCH 18, 1959 Hawaii becomes the last star on the Stars and Stripes, the 50th state of the union. The first jet airliners arrive, bringing 250,000 tourists to the fledgling state.

1960 Amfac, owner of Pioneer Sugar Company, builds Maui's first destination resort in Kaanapali.

1967 The state of Hawaii hosts 1 million tourists.

1975 Maui reaches the 1 million annual tourists mark. Ten years later the number is 2 million.

1990S Hawaii's state economy goes into a tailspin following a series of events: First, the Gulf War severely curtails air travel to the island; then, Hurricane Iniki slams into Kauai, crippling its infrastructure; and finally, sugar-cane companies across the state began shutting down, laying off thousands of workers. Maui, however, weathers this turbulent economic storm.

The Hawaiian **Language**

Almost everyone here speaks English. But many folks in Hawaii speak Hawaiian as well. All visitors will hear the words *aloha* (hello/goodbye/love) and *mahalo* (thank you). If you've just arrived, you're a *malihini*. Someone who's been here a long time is a *kamaaina*. When you finish a job or your meal, you are *pau* (finished). On Friday it's *pau hana,* work finished. You eat *pupu* (Hawaii's version of hors d'oeuvres) when you go *pau hana.*

The Hawaiian alphabet, created by the New England missionaries, has only 12 letters: the 5 regular vowels (a, e, i, o, and u) and 7 consonants (h, k, l, m, n, p, and w). The vowels are pronounced in the Roman fashion, that is, *ah, ay, ee, oh,* and *oo* (as in "too")—not *ay, ee, eye, oh,* and *you,* as in English. For example, *huhu* is pronounced *who-who.* Most vowels are sounded separately, though some are pronounced together, as in Kalakaua: *Kah-lah-cow-ah.*

WHAT HAOLE MEANS When Hawaiians first saw Western visitors, they called the pale-skinned, frail men *haole* because they looked so out of

breath. In Hawaiian, *ha* means *breath,* and *ole* means an absence of what precedes it. Today the term *haole* is generally a synonym for Caucasian or foreigner and is used without any intended disrespect. If uttered by an angry stranger who adds certain adjectives (like "stupid"), the term can be construed as a racial slur.

Useful Words & Phrases

Here are some basic Hawaiian words that you'll often hear in Hawaii and see throughout this book. For a more complete list of Hawaiian words, point your Web browser to www.geocities.com/~olelo/hltableof contents.html or www.hisurf.com/ hawaiian/dictionary.html.

alii   Hawaiian royalty

aloha   greeting or farewell

halau   school

hale   house or building

heiau   Hawaiian temple or place of worship

kahuna   priest or expert

kamaaina   old-timer

kapa   tapa, bark cloth

kapu   taboo, forbidden

keiki child
lanai porch or veranda
lomilomi massage
mahalo thank you
makai a direction, toward the sea
mana spirit power
mauka a direction, toward the mountains
muumuu loose-fitting gown or dress
ono delicious
pali cliff
paniolo Hawaiian cowboy(s)
wiki quick

Pidgin: 'Eh Fo'Real, Brah

If you venture beyond the tourist areas, you might hear another local tongue: pidgin English, a conglomeration of slang and words from the Hawaiian language. "Broke da mouth" (tastes really good) is the favorite pidgin phrase and one you might hear; "'Eh fo'real, brah" means "It's true, brother." You could be invited to hear an elder "talk story" (relating myths and memories). But because pidgin is really the province of the locals, your visit to Hawaii is likely to pass without your hearing much pidgin at all.

Eating in **Maui**

In the mid-1980s, Hawaii Regional Cuisine (HRC) ignited a culinary revolution. Culinary traditions from successive waves of Asian residents have resulted in unforgettable flavor combinations recalling Thai, Vietnamese, Japanese, Chinese, and Indo-Pacific roots. When combined with the fresh harvests from sea and land for which Hawaii is known, these ethnic and culinary traditions take on renewed vigor and a cross-cultural, yet uniquely Hawaiian, quality.

At the other end of the spectrum is the vast and endearing world of "local food." By that I mean plate lunches and poke, shave ice and *saimin*, *bento* lunches and *manapua*—cultural hybrids all. A **plate lunch** (Hawaii's version of high camp) is usually ordered from a lunch wagon and consists of fried mahimahi (or teriyaki beef or shoyu chicken), "two scoops rice," macaroni salad, and a few leaves of green, typically julienned cabbage. Heavy gravy is often the condiment of choice, accompanied by a soft drink in a paper cup or straight out of the can.

Another favorite is **saimin**—the local version of noodles in broth topped with scrambled eggs, green onions, and sometimes pork.

The **bento,** another popular quick meal available throughout Hawaii, is a compact, boxed assortment of picnic fare usually consisting of neatly arranged sections of rice, pickled vegetables, and fried chicken, beef, or pork.

From the plantations come **manapua,** a bready, doughy sphere filled with tasty fillings of sweetened pork or sweet beans. The daintier Chinese delicacy **dim sum** is made of translucent wrappers filled with fresh seafood, pork hash, and vegetables, served for breakfast and lunch. For dessert or a snack, the prevailing choice is **shave ice,** the island version of a snow cone.

A Hawaiian Seafood Primer

To help familiarize you with the menu language of Hawaii, here's a basic glossary of island fish:
ahi yellowfin or big-eye tuna
aku skipjack tuna
ehu red snapper
hapuupuu grouper, a sea bass
hebi spearfish
kajiki Pacific blue marlin, also called *au*

kumu   goatfish
mahimahi   dolphin fish (the game fish, not the mammal)
monchong   bigscale or sickle pomfret
nairagi   striped marlin, also called *au*
onaga   ruby snapper
ono   wahoo

opah   moonfish
opakapaka   pink snapper
papio   jack trevally
shutome   broadbill swordfish
tombo   albacore tuna
uhu   parrotfish
uku   gray snapper
ulua   large jack trevally

Toll-Free Numbers **& Websites**

Airlines on Maui

AIR CANADA
☎ 888/247-2262
www.aircanada.com

ALOHA AIRLINES
☎ 800/367-5250
www.alohaair.com

AMERICAN AIRLINES
☎ 800/433-7300
www.aa.com

AMERICAN TRANS AIR
☎ 800/435-9282
www.ata.com

AMERICAN WEST
☎ 800/327-7810
www.americanwest.com

CONTINENTAL AIRLINES
☎ 800/525-0280
www.continental.com

DELTA AIRLINES
☎ 800/221-1212
www.delta.com

GO!
☎ 888/IFLYGO2
www.iflygo.com

HARMONY AIRWAYS
☎ 866/868-6789
www.harmonyairways.com

HAWAIIAN AIRLINES
☎ 800/367-5320
www.hawaiianair.com

NORTHWEST AIRLINES
☎ 800/225-2525
www.nwa.com

SOUTHWEST AIRLINES
☎ 800/435-9792
www.southwest.com

UNITED AIRLINES
☎ 800/241-6522
www.ual.com

WEST JET
☎ 888/WESTJET
www.westjet.com

Car Rental Agencies on Maui

ALAMO
☎ 800/327-9633
www.goalamo.com

AVIS
☎ 800/321-3712
www.avis.com

BUDGET
☎ 800/572-0700
www.budget.com

DOLLAR
☎ 800/800-4000
www.dollarcar.com

HERTZ
☎ 800/654-3011
www.hertz.com

MAUI CRUISERS
☎ 877/749-7889
www.mauicruisers.net

NATIONAL
☎ 800/227-7368
www.nationalcar.com

WORD OF MOUTH RENT-A-USED-CAR
☎ 800/533-5929
www.mauirentacar.com

Index

See also Accommodations and Restaurant indexes, below.

Photo **Credits**

Jenny/Alamy; p 52, bottom: © Karl Lehmann/Lonely Planet Images; p 53, top: © Rough Guides/Alamy; p 53, bottom: © Elfi Kluck/Index Stock Imagery; p 55, top: © Cornforth Images/Alamy; p 56, bottom: © Tom Dove/Kealia Pond National Wildlife Refuge; p 57, top: © Jim Cazel/Photo Resource Hawaii/Alamy; p 59, top: © Andy Jackson/Alamy; p 62, top: © Charles Benes/Index Stock Imagery; p 63, bottom: Courtesy Bailey House Museum; p 65, top: © James Marshall/Lonely Planet Images; p 67, bottom: © Ann Cecil/Lonely Planet Images; p 68, bottom: © Russ Bishop/AGE Fotostock; p 69, top: © David Olsen/Photo Resource Hawaii/Alamy; p 69, bottom: © Douglas Peebles Photography/Alamy; p 71, middle: © Andy Jackson/Alamy; p 72, top: © Douglas Peebles/AGE Fotostock; p 73, bottom: © SuperStock/AGE Fotostock; p 74, top: © SuperStock/AGE Fotostock; p 74, bottom: © Koa Kahili/Index Stock Imagery; p 75: © Douglas Peebles/eStock Photo; p 76, bottom: © Super-Stock/AGE Fotostock; p 78, bottom: © Peter French/Index Stock Imagery; p 79, top: © Andy Jackson/Alamy; p 80, top: © David Olsen/Alamy; p 80, bottom: © Brent Bergherm/AGE Fotostock; p 81, top: © James Hackett/eStock Photo; p 82, top: © Douglas Peebles/eStock Photo; p 83: © David Fleetham/Alamy; p 85, bottom: © G. Brad Lewis/Photo Resource Hawaii/Alamy; p 86, bottom: © Jim Cazel/Photo Resource Hawaii/Alamy; p 87, top: © Ann Cecil/Lonely Planet Images; p 89, bottom: © Omni Photo Communications Inc./Index Stock Imagery; p 91, top: © SuperStock/AGE Fotostock; p 94, bottom: © SIME s.a.s./eStock Photo; p 95, top: © Marc Schechter/Photo Resource Hawaii/Alamy; p 97, bottom: © Lee Foster/Lonely Planet Images; p 98, top: © David Fleetham/Alamy; p 99, bottom: Courtesy Skyline Eco-Adventures; p 101, bottom: © Ron Dahlquist/SuperStock; p 102, top: © Casey Mahaney/Lonely Planet Images; p 105, bottom: © Bill Brooks/Alamy; p 106, top: © Eric Sanford/Index Stock Imagery; p 107, bottom: © David Fleetham/Alamy; p 108, bottom: © Michael S. Nolan/AGE Fotostock; p 109: Courtesy Fairmont Kea Lani Maui; p 110, bottom: Courtesy Kaanapali Beach Hotel; p 115, top: © David Franzen/Photo Resource Hawaii/Alamy; p 115, bottom: © SIME s.a.s./eStock Photo; p 116, bottom: © Franco Salmoiraghi/Photo Resource Hawaii/Alamy; p 117, top: Courtesy Kapalua Resort; p 118, bottom: © Tony Novak-Clifford/Courtesy Napili Kai Beach Resort; p 119: © Kent S. Hwang/Courtesy David Paul's Lahaina Grill; p 120, bottom: Courtesy The Pineapple Grill; p 125, top: Courtesy Old Lahaina Luau; p 126, bottom: © Kent S. Hwang/Courtesy David Paul's Lahaina Grill; p 126, top: ©Steve Brinkman/Bev Gannon Restaurants; p 127, top: © Steve Brinkman/Courtesy Roselani Ice Cream; p 128, bottom: © Tony Novak-Clifford Photography/Courtesy Mama's Fish House; p 129, top: Courtesy The Pineapple Grill; p 129, bottom: Courtesy Roy's Kahana Bar & Grill; p 130, top: Courtesy Sansei Seafood Restaurant & Sushi Bar; p 130, bottom: © Steve Brinkman/Courtesy Vino Italian Tapas and Wine; p 131: © Jeff Greenberg/Index Stock Imagery; p 132, bottom: Courtesy Maui Ocean Center; p 137, bottom: Courtesy Sig Zane Kaiao; p 138, bottom: Courtesy Kii Gallery; p 139, top: © Sherri Reeve Gallery and Gifts; p 140, top: Courtesy Maggie Coulombe; p 141, bottom: Courtesy Maui Ocean Center; p 142, bottom: Courtesy Kii Gallery; p 143: Courtesy Old Lahaina Luau; p 144, middle: © Douglas Peebles Photography/Alamy; p 149, top: Courtesy Maui Film Festival; p 149, bottom: © Tony Novak-Clifford/Courtesy Maui Arts & Culture Center; p 150, bottom: Courtesy Hawaiian Slack Key Guitar Productions; p 150, top: Courtesy Old Lahaina Luau; p 151: © Karl Lehmann/Lonely Planet Images; p 153, bottom: © Ann Cecil/Lonely Planet Images; p 154, top: © Ann Cecil/Lonely Planet Images; p 154: © David Schrichte/Photo Resource Hawaii/Alamy; p 155, top: © Andre Jenny/Alamy; p 157, bottom: © Walter Bibikow/Index Stock Imagery; p 158, top: © David Schrichte/Photo Resource Hawaii/Alamy; p 159, bottom: © Karl Lehmann/Lonely Planet Images; p 161: © Blaine Harrington/AGE Fotostock.

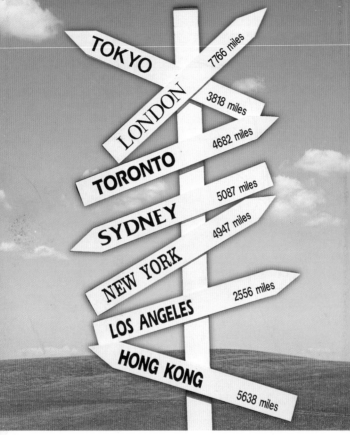

Explore over 3,500 destinations.

Frommers.com makes it easy.

Find a destination. ✓ Book a trip. ✓ Get hot travel deals.
Buy a guidebook. ✓ Enter to win vacations. ✓ Listen to podcasts.
Check out the latest travel news. ✓ Share trip photos and memories.
And much more.

Frommers.com